ENVIRONMENTAL CONCERNS

Peter Alma
Senior Lecturer in Ecology
Worcester College of Higher Education

 **CAMBRIDGE**
UNIVERSITY PRESS

Published by the Press Syndicate of the University of Cambridge
The Pitt Building, Trumpington Street, Cambridge CB2 1RP
40 West 20th Street, New York, NY 10011-4211, USA
10 Stamford Road, Oakleigh, Melbourne 3166, Australia

First published 1993

Printed in Great Britain at the University Press, Cambridge

A catalogue record for this book is available from the British Library

ISBN 0 521 42869 6 paperback

Cover photo: Flames from burning oil wells, Kuwait: Peter Menzel/Science
Photo Library

Text illustrations by Chris Etheridge

Contents

Preface

This book is intended to be used in schools but would also serve as an introductory text for those interested in the environment in which we live. Much of the material is derived from lecture courses that I give to undergraduates at Worcester College of Higher Education.

The book examines environmental problems of the present day from the perspective of an ecologist concerned with impacts of human activities on the integrity of ecosystem function, energy flow and nutrient cycling. Global and local issues receive consideration and the impact of land-use changes, forestry operations and human pressures on semi-arid regions are assessed. The exploitation, conservation and management of biological systems forms a significant part of the second half of the book. The concluding chapter explores the principles and practice of reclaiming derelict land.

I am aware that it is not possible to be an expert on all the subjects covered in this text. I have depended very much, therefore, on the work of others and I am, accordingly, grateful for their painstaking research and hard work. I hope that, in selecting the material and distilling it into this form, I have not been guilty of misrepresentation or error. Furthermore, I hope that I will be forgiven if I have inadvertently cast my words in a form close to that of others.

I would like to thank Alan Cornwell and Cambridge University Press for the invitation to write this book and assisting me in its production. Dr C.J. Betts of Christopher Betts Consulting and Applied Ecologists kindly helped search for material for the book and commented on drafts. Finally I am very grateful to my wife Valerie and to my children who worked hard to help me with this task.

Environmental concerns having global impacts

1.1 Biogeochemical cycles

To understand the significance of some of the factors which cause environmental concerns, particularly on a global scale, it is necessary to understand biogeochemical cycles. **Biogeochemical cycles** are models of the position and behaviour of materials, usually elements or compounds, on a local or global scale under the influence of living organisms, physical earth processes and chemical earth processes. It is possible to distinguish between three types of cycle:

1 Local cycles involve the less mobile elements and have no mechanism of long-distance transport. They are characterised by the absence of leakage from one ecosystem to another. Examples of elements that participate in local cycles are phosphorus (P), potassium (K), calcium (Ca), magnesium (Mg), copper (Cu), zinc (Zn), boron (B), molybdenum (Mo), manganese (Mn) and iron (Fe).
2 Global cycles have a gaseous component which allows the element or compound to be transported over great distances in the atmosphere. This includes elements and compounds which may also participate, in a different state, in local cycles. Elements of significance here are carbon (C), oxygen (O), hydrogen (H), sulphur (S) and nitrogen (N), often in a variety of gaseous compounds (e.g. carbon dioxide (CO_2), water (H_2O), oxides of nitrogen (NO_x), methane (CH_4), sulphur dioxide (SO_2)).
3 Sedimentary cycles, in which particulate material of all sorts is transported by water or sometimes wind.

It is usual for biogeochemical cycles to be described in model form with two components:

1 Biogeochemical pools (pools for short) are the quantities of the chemical being modelled in a recognisable portion of the globe or ecosystem (e.g. the atmosphere, the soil, phytoplankton).
2 Transfer rates (or fluxes) are the rates of transfer of the chemical from one pool to another.

This can be understood more easily by examining real models. Two examples, phosphorus and carbon, are given below.

The local **cycling of phosphorus** based on data from a study in a mature stand of maple–birch woodland (*Acer saccharum–Acer rubrum–Betula allegheniensis*) in Nova Scotia, Canada, is shown in figure 1.1. As this particular model uses information from several studies, the overall balance of the model can be taken as an approximation only. It does show, however, that phosphorus is relatively immobile, an important feature of this element's behaviour when it comes to examining its role in environmental problems. This model is not too complex, and because its data are derived from studies of small areas, the units used to express pool size and transfer rates are comprehensible.

The global biogeochemical **cycle of carbon** has some disagreement about sizes of pools and transfer rates, and the units used to express pool sizes (billion tonnes) are almost beyond grasp (all in contrast to phosphorus). One carbon model which appears to have gained a reasonable degree of acceptance is shown in figure 1.2. The interesting features here are:

1 The huge size of the pool of carbon in sediments, 20 million billion tonnes.
2 Fossil fuel combustion is removing carbon from the coal and oil pool much faster than it is being added to.
3 Despite the small size of the phytoplankton pool (5 billion tonnes), the flux of carbon out of this pool (40 billion tonnes year^{-1} into dead organic matter and consumption by zooplankton and fish) is larger than that (25 billion tonnes year^{-1}) from the plants on land (pool size 450 tonnes). This is because the turnover time (or life-cycle) of phytoplankton is so rapid.
4 Transfer rates into and out of the atmosphere (almost entirely carbon dioxide) are very high compared to the relatively small size of the pool. Residence time of carbon in the atmosphere is thus low.

The interest in biogeochemical cycles lies in the way pool sizes and transfer rates of a variety of elements and compounds, and nutrients and toxins have been influenced in ways which cause environmental problems. Environmental concerns arise when local or global biogeochemical cycles are opened or their pathways diverted or dominated by human activity. It is necessary, therefore, to have a mental picture of these cycles when considering these concerns.

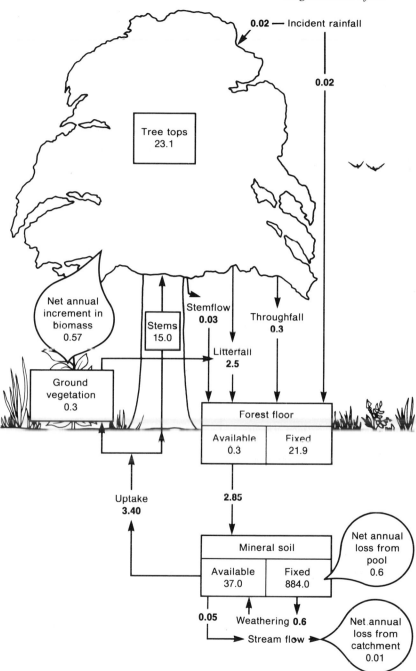

Figure 1.1 Generalised model for the local biogeochemical cycling of phosphorus in maple–birch woodland in Nova Scotia: standing crops = pools (in boxes) are in kg ha^{-1}, transfer rates (on arrows) are in kg ha^{-1} year^{-1}. (Data from Freedman (1989).)

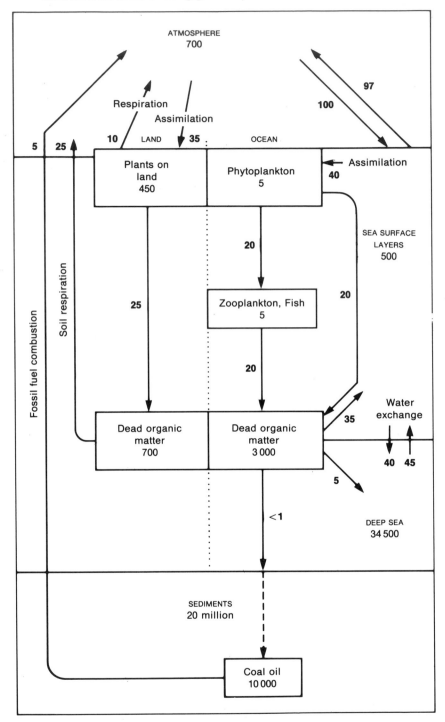

Figure 1.2 Model of global carbon flow: pool sizes are in billion metric tonnes, transfer rates (on arrows) are in billion metric tonnes year^{-1}. (Data from Bolin B. (1970) in *Scientific American* **223**:124–32.)

1.2   Ozone depletion

Ozone (O_3) is not an abundant chemical in the atmosphere, but it is highly significant because of several important properties:

1 It absorbs ultraviolet light (UV light).
2 It is involved in a complex series of chemical interactions with natural and pollutant chemicals in the atmosphere.
3 It has harmful effects on living organisms.

Ozone's capacity for absorbing UV light in the stratosphere is discussed here. Because the effects of ozone relate very much to its vertical distribution pattern in the atmosphere, it is essential that the terminology of the layers of the atmosphere is understood (see figure 1.3). The concentration of most atmospheric gases is highest at the earth's surface and declines in more or less a linear fashion with altitude. Ozone is aberrant, with an unusually high concentration in the stratosphere, where it acts as a filter for incoming UV radiation. Ozone is produced in this layer by the dissociation of oxygen, a reaction which occurs in the presence of UV light (wavelengths 180–240 nm):

$$O_2 + hv \rightarrow O + O$$

$$O + O_2 \rightarrow O_3$$

(hv is the symbol for a quantum of energy, here derived from UV light.)

It is thought that most of the ozone is produced in equatorial regions, where UV radiation penetrates furthest into the atmosphere, and is then transported around the globe by stratospheric air currents. The ozone is also converted back to oxygen by slightly longer wavelength UV light (200–320 nm). Absorption of UV light by these two reactions screens out a part of the light spectrum that is harmful to living organisms and warms the stratosphere. It is probably this action, producing the high ozone concentrations at about 23–30 km, which accounts for the high temperature of the stratosphere at this level. The balance between production and destruction of ozone normally keeps a relatively constant level of the gas in the stratosphere.

High intensities of UV light cause a variety of problems for biological systems. The wavelengths of UV light between 290 nm and 320 nm damage biological molecules, amino acids, proteins and nucleic acids, and consequently cells and tissues. The cells of the surfaces of living organisms exposed to UV light are at risk from damage, disruption of physiological processes, and scrambling of their genetic code. Exposure to high levels of UV light causes sunburn, it accelerates ageing of the skin, it suppresses the immune response, and long exposure to bright sunlight is implicated in increasing the incidence of skin cancer in humans and other animals. The

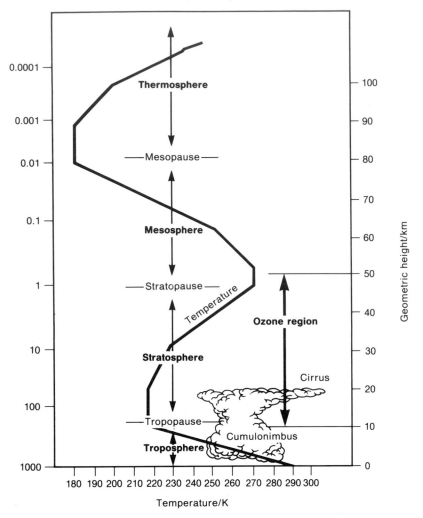

Figure 1.3 The layers of the atmosphere and its temperature profile. The region of ozone is between altitudes of approximately 10 km and 50 km.

incidences of skin cancer in Caucasoids are much higher in countries where the sky is clear for long periods and the intensity of sunlight is high, for example in Australia, New Zealand and South Africa. The indigenous people of these countries have dark skins, which filter out UV light. Plant tissue is also susceptible to UV radiation. Biochemical composition of tissues and photosynthesis are affected.

The ozone layer of the stratosphere of Antarctica has been studied since 1957 by the British Antarctic Survey. The depth of the ozone layer at the poles is greater than at the equator. In 1982 the Survey noticed, for the first time, a depletion in the layer in October, the southern hemisphere spring. The data for October, from the time measurements were first taken,

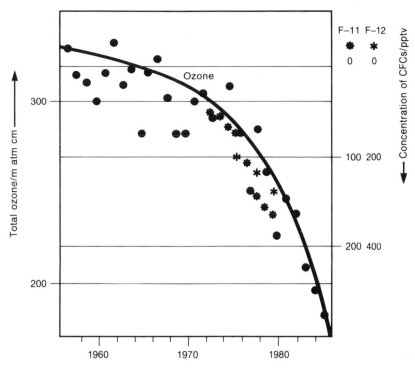

Figure 1.4 Ozone concentration in the atmosphere over the Antarctic (Halley Bay) in October. The concentrations of two chlorofluorocarbons (CFCs) are also shown: note the axis for their concentrations is inverted. (Redrawn from Farman J. (1987) in *New Scientist* 12 November:50–4.)

showed that a dramatic decline in ozone levels had commenced in about 1970. This coincided with an increase in the level of chlorofluorocarbons (CFCs) in the atmosphere (see figure 1.4). CFCs had been predicted, in the early 1970s, to be likely to release free chlorine atoms when they reached and then decomposed in the stratosphere. These chlorine atoms were known to be capable of destroying ozone molecules and, in the process, releasing the active chlorine atom again. This reaction is intensified by the presence of ice crystals and is believed to be the reason why ozone depletion occurs first at the poles. (A second reason is that ozone may be broken down faster than it can be replaced, as maximum ozone production occurs in the tropics.)

CFCs are used as refrigerants and aerosol propellants. There is now little doubt that the serious depletion of atmospheric ozone is strongly influenced by CFC gases. Owing to the concern over atmospheric ozone depletion, considerable strides have been made in the substitution of CFCs with 'ozone-friendly' refrigerants and propellants. Other chemicals have been found to act in a similar way to CFCs; nitrogen oxide (NO) produced from dinitrogen oxide (N_2O) in the stratosphere also destroys ozone. A simple diagram illustrates the atmospheric gas flows in these reactions (see

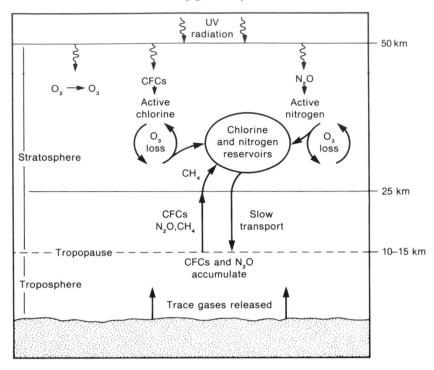

Figure 1.5 The pathways leading to the breakdown of stratospheric ozone. The gases involved move slowly into the stratosphere where they are broken down by UV light into ozone-destroying catalysts. (Adapted from Warr K. (1990) in *New Scientist* 27 October:36–40.)

figure 1.5). This model also alerts us to the fact that many of the chemicals involved in ozone destruction are industrially produced and have a long retention time in the stratosphere. Reductions in production of these gases now will have little impact on their concentrations in the stratosphere for a long time. About one-third of one CFC ($CFCl_3$, known as F–11) present in 1987 will remain in the stratosphere in 65 years time, and for a second (CF_2Cl_2, F–12) the equivalent time will be 120 years. It would be necessary to cut CFC emissions to about 15% of their 1987 levels to prevent increases in atmospheric concentrations of these gases in the future.

The reduction of ozone levels in the stratosphere over Antarctica has been described, popularly, as the **ozone hole**, owing to a virtual absence of ozone. Depressions of up to 50% of normal ozone concentrations, lasting 30–40 days in spring were noted in the late 1980s and appear to be becoming greater. Atmospheric circulation around the Arctic and other aspects of its meteorology are much more complex than in Antarctica. Because of this, conditions for ozone depletion are less likely to occur in the northern hemisphere, but an **ozone crater** (a less severe central depletion zone than a hole) was first reported in the Arctic in 1989.

The industrialised nations have limited the production and use of CFCs in response to this concern. On 16 September 1987, an initiative of the United Nations Environment Programme which began in 1973 was concluded when 21 states and those of the European Community (EC) signed the Montreal Protocol. This is a three-phase programme of objectives for reducing CFC production:

Phase 1. Nations were to cap CFC production in the middle of the year at 1986 levels.
Phase 2. Between mid-1993 and 1994 nations should cut CFC consumption by 20%.
Phase 3. By 1999 CFC use should be reduced by 50%.

There were exemptions for some Eastern Bloc countries, developing countries, Brazil and Argentina. Given the persistence of CFCs in the atmosphere, many scientists working in this field think that this is an inadequate reduction. There is evidence to show that CFC levels will still be increasing in 1999, even if consumption is cut to 50% of 1986 levels. The protocol is reviewed periodically.

1.3   Acid rain

The term 'acid rain' was first used by Robert Angus Smith in 1872 when, as Chief Alkali Inspector of the UK, he described acidity of the polluted rain falling around Manchester. Distilled water has a pH of 7.0, but unpolluted rainfall, which contains dissolved carbon dioxide (carbonic acid), has a pH of 5.65. This can be modified by naturally occurring chemicals, for example hydrogen sulphide from hot springs, sulphur dioxide from volcanic eruptions and a variety of chemicals derived from soil particles. Any form of wet precipitation, including rainfall, snow and condensing fog, with a pH lower than 5.6 is referred to as acid precipitation or, more commonly, **acid rain**. Pollutants responsible for acidification of our environment are also deposited by gravity and by contact with surfaces. These dry deposited pollutants can have direct effects on the surfaces to which they adhere, but also contribute to acidification of waters when they interact with rainfall.

Examination of past precipitation captured as a historical record in ice sheets and glaciers has indicated that its pH prior to the Industrial Revolution was between 5.0 and 6.0. The average pHs of rainfall in parts of Europe and the USA are now below 5.0 or even 4.0. Exceptionally low values (e.g. pH 2.4 at Pitlochry, Scotland, in 1974) have been recorded in some rainstorms. The pollutants that are reponsible for this acidification are oxides of nitrogen and sulphur, which ultimately produce nitric and sulphuric acids. In some areas (e.g. north-eastern USA) hydrochloric acid (HCl) is also significant. The increasing levels of acidity in rain are a serious problem because of their impact on soil nutrients and the health of forests, agricultural crops and freshwater habitats. The problems are more severe near and downwind of large centres of population and their attendant industries, for example in north-eastern North America, central Europe and Scandinavia.

1.4   Origins of the acids

Oxides of nitrogen and acid rain

The reactions which produce nitric acid (HNO_3) from oxides of nitrogen in the atmosphere are very complicated and are modified by temperature, light conditions and the presence of particulate matter and hydrocarbons in the air. Any process which leads to an increase in nitric acid in the atmosphere will decrease the pH of atmospheric precipitation.

Nitrogen oxide (NO) is an important precursor in the atmospheric generation of nitric acid. It has been estimated that of the atmospheric oxides of nitrogen about 30% are derived from internal combustion engines, 45% from power-generating plants and 25% from domestic and general industrial sources. Nitrogen oxide interacts with ozone (O_3), oxygen (O_2) and energy-absorbing surfaces to produce an equilibrium mixture of nitrogen oxide, nitrogen dioxide (NO_2) and ozone. A further set of reactions converts nitrogen dioxide into nitric acid, which in turn can also be broken down in the atmosphere.

The most abundant oxide of nitrogen in the atmosphere is dinitrogen oxide (N_2O), most of which arrives in the atmosphere via microbial denitrification in anaerobic conditions. Nitrate ions (NO_3^-) are used by denitrifying soil microbes instead of oxygen for respiration and are reduced to produce nitrogen gas (N_2) and dinitrogen oxide. Applications of nitrate fertilisers to waterlogged or compacted soil encourage denitrification, thus wasting money through loss of nutrients. Dinitrogen oxide is relatively stable and is persistent in the atmosphere. If it enters the stratosphere it can decompose either into nitrogen and oxygen or react with atomic oxygen in the presence of bright sunlight to produce nitrogen oxide. Nitrogen oxide is involved in reactions which reduce ozone levels in the stratosphere.

Sulphur compounds and acid rain

Sulphur (S) can enter the atmosphere through a variety of routes, principally as sulphur dioxide (SO_2) from the burning of fossil fuels (coal, oils, natural gas), and refined diesel and petrol hydrocarbons. Approximately half the input of sulphur dioxide into the atmosphere is thought to be natural. Whereas the natural input is global, the rest is concentrated in industrialised parts of the world. The problem with sulphur dioxide is that it is oxidised to produce sulphuric acid and adds to the acidification of falling rain. The chemistry of transformation of the pollutant to the acid is complex. Sulphur dioxide gas interacts with water in cloud droplets to produce bisulphite (HSO_3^-) and sulphite (SO_3^{2-}) ions. These are oxidised in solution in cloud droplets by a variety of atmospheric chemicals to produce sulphuric acid (sulphate (SO_4^{2-}) and hydrogen (H^+) ions). It appears that the oxidant most important in controlling acid production is cloudwater hydrogen peroxide (H_2O_2). Some atmospheric sulphur dioxide is absorbed by vegetation and into the surface of oceans, but most is thought to be converted to sulphuric acid.

A second significant route by which sulphur enters the atmosphere is as dimethyl sulphide (($(CH_3)_2S$), a volatile organic chemical produced in large quantities by decomposition of plankton in the oceans. Dimethyl sulphide accounts for about half of the gaseous sulphur (approximately 200 million tonnes) that circulates through the atmosphere each year. A mechanism for its conversion to sulphuric acid in the presence of other atmospheric pollutants has been proposed.

1.5 Acid rainfall

Acid rain falls when the acids in the atmosphere reach the ground through the action of **washout** (when the acids present below clouds are taken up by falling rain or snow) or **rainout** (when the cloudwater droplets or ice crystals containing the acids grow to sufficient size to fall). The gaseous precursors of acid rain are capable of being distributed on a global scale. It is found, however, that as the sources of the gases are centred on industrial countries the greatest effects of acid rain are experienced in areas downwind of these sources (see figure 1.6). South-westerly winds in Europe carry aerial pollutants from western Europe into central and northern Europe. It has been estimated that the UK is the source for about 16% of the acid rain falling in southern Norway. Although airstreams originating from the UK do reach Scandinavia, the air is only mildly polluted compared with the highly acidic rainfall that falls there which originates from airstreams flowing from Czechoslovakia, Hungary, Poland and Germany. It is interesting to compare the proportions of locally produced and imported pollutants in European countries (see table 1.1).

Countries such as Switzerland and Norway contribute little to their own sulphur deposition, lacking the advantage of being a western European state (e.g. UK and Spain) in a region of the world with prevailing westerly winds. The Scandinavians are in an invidious position: with low population density and relatively low sulphur emissions, they receive a high proportion of 'imported' sulphur from elsewhere.

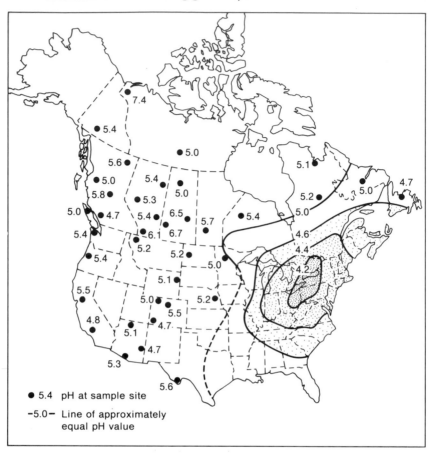

Figure 1.6 The pH of rainfall in North America in 1982. Downwind of the industrialised regions, the pH is much lower. (Redrawn from Miller J. M. (1984) in *Weatherwise* **37**:222–51.)

Table 1.1. Estimated sulphur sources as a percentage of the total deposition within selected European countries, October 1978 to September 1980

	Foreign sources	Indigenous sources	Undecided background deposition
Czechoslovakia	56	37	7
Denmark	54	36	10
Finland	55	26	19
France	34	52	14
East Germany	32	65	3
West Germany	45	48	7
Hungary	54	42	4
Netherlands	71	23	6

Table 1.1. (cont.)

	Foreign sources	Indigenous sources	Undecided background deposition
Norway	63	8	29
Poland	52	42	6
Spain	18	63	19
Sweden	58	18	24
Switzerland	78	10	12
UK	12	79	12

Source: EMEP. The co-operative programme for monitoring and evaluation of long-range transmission of air pollution in Europe, *Economic Bulletin for Europe,* United Nations Economic Commission for Europe (UN/ECE) **34**:29–40.

1.6 History of acidification

Studies have been made of diatoms in sediments of lakes and, with a knowledge of the pH preferences of the species discovered, it has been possible to estimate pH levels in lake waters over long periods of time. The pH of the water in Lake Gardsjon, Sweden, had declined from about pH 7.0, 12 500 years ago to pH 6.0 in the mid-1950s as a result of natural processes after the last glacial retreat. From about the mid-1950s to 1979 the pH of the lake fell from 6.0 to 4.5. This pattern has been found elsewhere. In the last fifty years or so, pH values have rapidly changed. However, it is not known why the impact of acid emissions (polluted outpourings initially produced at the beginning of the Industrial Revolution over 200 years ago) has taken so long to manifest itself in lake waters. It may have taken this period of time for the capacity of the environment to absorb the hydrogen ions to be saturated. The problems being seen in Scandinavian lakes and central European forests in the 1990s are the consequences of decades, if not centuries, of pollution.

The contributions of sulphuric and nitric acids to acid rain vary according to the locality (see table 1.2). There is a trend towards an

Table 1.2. Contributions (%) of nitric, sulphuric and hydrochloric acid to acid rain in different parts of the world

	Acid species		
	Nitric	Sulphuric	Hydrochloric
Northern USA	32	62	6
Scandinavia	30	70	NA
Scotland	29	71	NA

NA   Data not available

increasing proportion of the acidity being derived from nitric acid as the burning of fossil fuels continues to increase.

1.7 Impact of acid rain

The impact of acid rain on soils and water depend on the capacity of the minerals in the soil and the catchment of lakes and rivers to absorb hydrogen ions without significant changes in pH or in the behaviour of soil nutrients (i.e. the environment's **buffering capacity**). Soils derived from sedimentary rocks with high levels of calcium and magnesium have good buffering properties. Those formed on igneous or metamorphic rocks are strongly influenced by acid rain and exhibit a proportionately greater acidification for the same input of hydrogen ions (i.e. poor buffering capacity). This has been one of the main reasons why the effects of acid rain have been so evident in southern Scandinavia, in upland areas in the UK and in parts of Canada where the soils are derived from granite or are sandy.

Acid rain causes problems in soils in various ways. Low pH leads to leaching of some nutrients (e.g. Ca, Mg and K), increases the solubility of others (e.g. Al, Fe and Mn), mobilises toxic metals ions (e.g. Pb and Ni) and immobilises some important nutrients (e.g. Mo). Low pHs inhibit decomposition by bacteria and fungi. The low calcium levels found in acid soils exclude earthworms and molluscs, whose acitivity is important in decomposition processes. One of the most significant changes that occurs in soil is the release of aluminium ions into soil solution. Aluminium in solution has been shown to be toxic to plants, and to reduce the uptake of calcium and probably other cations. Acid rain has been linked with growth problems in forests in Canada and Europe that appear to be due to deficiencies of potassium and magnesium and to changes in the balance between calcium and aluminium ions in soil solution.

In freshwater ecosystems the impact of excess hydrogen and toxic aluminium ions in water can be catastrophic. In southern Norway it was estimated that in 1983 lakes of a total surface area of 13 000 km^2 had no fish. In parallel to this there has been an increase in the proportion of Scandinavian lakes which have lost their populations of brown trout (*Salmo trutta*) (see figure 1.7). Several lochs in Scotland and upland rivers in Britain are also without fish as a result of acidification.

Fish are killed because they lose ions from their plasma and muscle tissue in acid water. Aluminium ions cause excessive mucus production by the gill surfaces, which become clogged, eventually causing respiratory distress and death. Species richness of aquatic organisms declines with decreasing pH. This is well illustrated by the pH tolerance of common snails, mussels and crustaceans in some Norwegian lakes (see figure 1.8). Levels of pH well below 4.5 are not uncommon in acidified lakes and it is hardly

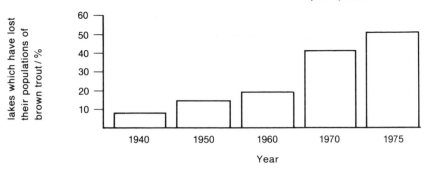

Figure 1.7 Changes in the proportion of lakes in Scandinavia which have lost their brown trout (*Salmo trutta*). (Data from Wellburn A. (1988).)

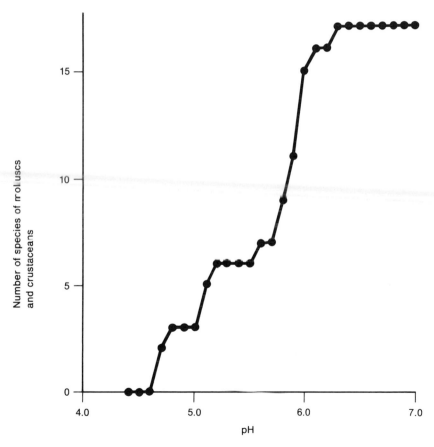

Figure 1.8 The pH tolerance of 27 common species of molluscs and crustaceans found in near-neutral waters in Norway. (Adapted from Økland J. & Økland K. A. (1980) in Drablos D. & Tollan A. (eds.) *Ecological impact of acid precipitation*, SNSF Project, Oslo.)

surprising they are almost devoid of life. Lake bottoms become covered with growths of acid-tolerant plants, a few species of green algae and moss.

As far as humans are concerned, the effects of high hydrogen and aluminium ion concentrations in drinking water are not well known. High aluminium levels in water supplies have been associated by epidemiological studies with increased incidences of a rare bone-wasting disease (osteo-malacia) and Alzheimer's disease (premature senile dementia). The possible relationship between aluminium and Alzheimer's disease is discussed by A. Cornwell and V. Cornwell in their book *Drugs, alcohol and mental health* (Cambridge University Press, 1993) in this series. High nitrate levels in water are known to cause methaemoglobinaemia in infants. The nitrates are converted to nitrites in infant guts, which, in contrast to adults, are not able to reduce nitrites to nitrogen. The nitrite combines, irreversibly, with haemoglobin, which can then no longer transport oxygen. Babies turn blue (blue-baby syndrome), suffer from respiratory distress, and may die. A link has been proposed between high nitrate levels and the incidence of stomach cancer arising from the production of nitroso compounds in the body from the nitrates. The link has not been proven, but nitroso compounds are known to be carcinogenic.

The high nitrate levels in lakes and groundwaters are derived from nitrate leaching from agricultural land as well as acid rain (see chapter 2). The fertilising effects of both sulphate and nitrate from acid rain has been shown to increase agricultural and forestry productivity until a point is reached where the increasing hydrogen ion concentrations become damaging (see chapter 2).

1.8   Reduction of the impact of acid rain

Acid rain is a serious problem. It warrants effective control but this cannot be achieved by treating symptoms. The problem must be solved by removing its causes. Further additions of nitrogen oxides and sulphur dioxide to the atmosphere can be reduced in a variety of ways.

1   Improved engine designs

The amounts of nitrogen oxide produced by burning fossil fuels in power stations, furnaces and motor engines can be reduced by careful design of fuel delivery, combustion chambers, exhaust systems and the way in which the machinery is operated. In cars, for example, the considerable strides made in improving engine design (computerised fuel injection and the lean-burn engine with its high air-to-fuel ratio) have been linked with improvements in exhaust treatment (exhaust recirculation, and three-way catalytic conver-sion, where carbon monoxide, unburned hydrocarbon and nitrogen oxide gases are eliminated) to provide considerable reduction in nitrogen oxide emission from exhausts. The changes in design have not all been associated with improving engine performance!

2 Low sulphur and cleansed fuels

The greatest proportion of the sulphur dioxide entering the atmosphere is produced by coal and oil burning. The sulphur content of coal and oil varies considerably (about 0.5% to 5.0%) and utilisation of low-sulphur coal and oil can help reduce emissions. Oil and coal fuels can also be cleansed, at least partly, of their sulphur content, but using low-sulphur fuels and cleansing alone is unlikely to be sufficient to meet emission-reduction targets of 50% within ten years.

The fluidised-bed combustion system for burning fuels in power stations is effective in reducing sulphur dioxide and nitrogen oxide emissions. Small particles (or droplets) of fuels are held suspended in a jet of air and burned at relatively low temperatures (500–900 °C) in the presence of ground limestone or dolomite. The low temperatures greatly reduce the production of nitrogen oxide and up to 90% of the sulphur is removed as magnesium or calcium sulphate in the ash. Table 1.3 compares the level of pollutant gases in emissions and the thermal efficiencies of five different power station systems, showing the gains that can be made by using the fluidised-bed system.

The quantities of sulphur dioxide emitted from power station exhaust chimneys can be reduced still further by flue gas desulphurisation systems, usually referred to as scrubbers. A slurry of lime or limestone is directed against the emerging flue gases and can remove 90–99% of flue gas sulphur dioxide. The byproduct of the process, gypsum, can be used in the manufacture of cement products.

Table 1.3. Thermal efficiency and emission qualities of power station combustion systems

		Gas emissions		
Combustion	% maximum thermal efficiency	Carbon monoxide	Sulphur dioxide	Nitrogen oxides
Oil-fired	35–37	trace	high	considerable
Natural gas-fired	35–37	trace	low	very high
Coal-fired	35–40	low	high	considerable
Gas turbine	18–28	high	very high	very high
Fluidised-bed	50–70	trace	low	low

Source: Wellburn (1988).

3 Liming

The symptoms of acidification of lakes and their catchment areas, and perhaps the decades of acidification past, can be treated by the application of lime. This will neutralise acidity, increase calcium levels in soil and water and precipitate aluminium from solution. This treatment has been used in Norway, Sweden, Canada, USA and the UK. It has been successful with some lakes but not all. Liming can cause significant changes to the terrestrial vegetation and to the living organisms in streams and lakes, which may be equally as unacceptable as the water's acidity.

1.9 Greenhouse effect

The temperature of the Earth's atmosphere is governed by many factors, but is essentially a product of the interaction of incoming solar radiation with a variety of compounds in the atmosphere. The temperature of the sun's surface is about $6000\,°C$ and it radiates most of its energy in the visible waveband (0.4–$0.7\,\mu m$). This penetrates the atmosphere and reaches the Earth's surface, along with some UV light (below $0.4\,\mu m$) and short wavelength infrared light (just above $0.7\,\mu m$). This warms the Earth's surface which then, because it is much cooler, radiates energy in the long infrared wavelengths (4–$100\,\mu m$). About 70% of this energy escapes into space, but some is absorbed by compounds in the atmosphere. Water vapour absorbs wavelengths from $4\,\mu m$ to $7\,\mu m$ and carbon dioxide absorbs from $7\,\mu m$ to $13\,\mu m$. This absorption of heat warms the troposphere (the atmosphere's lowest layer) and heat is radiated back and warms the Earth's surface. This is the **greenhouse effect**. Water vapour and carbon dioxide, and some other gases which have similar properties in this respect, are known as **greenhouse gases**. If the sun's heat supply to the Earth remains constant (which it does, more or less) and the concentration of greenhouse gases remains constant, then the heat balance of the atmosphere and the surface would be constant. One of our most serious global concerns is that the concentrations of greenhouse gases are not constant. They are being increased substantially by human activities (or anthropogenic influences), and there is undoubtedly a parallel rise in the temperature of the atmosphere.

1.10 Carbon dioxide as a greenhouse gas

Carbon dioxide levels in the atmosphere have been increasing for a long time. Data produced at the Mauna Loa Observatory, Hawaii, have shown an increase since records commenced in 1958. Data on levels of gases captured in ice cores suggest that carbon dioxide levels have fluctuated widely since the last glacial retreat, but they appear to be higher now than at any time since the last glaciation. It is clear that the present upward trend has gone on

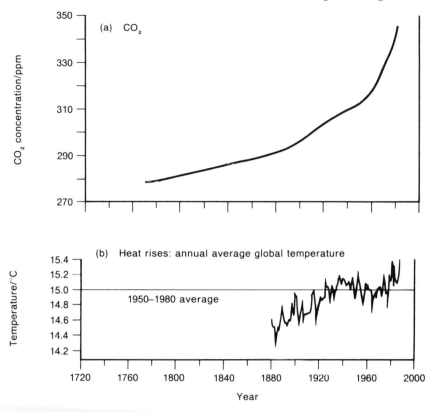

Figure 1.9 Changes in the atmosphere (*a*) global carbon dioxide concentrations since the Industrial Revolution and (*b*) temperature since 1880. (Data from Neftel A. *et al.* (1985) in *Nature* **315**:45–7; and Gribbin J. (1988) in *New Scientist* **120**.)

for 200 years at least (see figure 1.9). Research has also shown a close correlation between atmospheric carbon dioxide levels and global temperature. The carbon dioxide increase in the atmosphere represents a balance between the amount given off by respiration, burning of fossil fuels and forest conversion, on the one hand, and photosynthetic uptake and solution in the seas, on the other. The equation is not in balance now because the rate of carbon dioxide production from fossil fuels and forest conversion exceeds its fixation rate. It is estimated (early 1990s) that deforestation releases about 1–3 billion tonnes and the burning of fossil fuels 6 billion tonnes of carbon dioxide each year. Levels of carbon dioxide, about 350 ppm in the early 1990s, are expected to be in excess of 400 ppm by the turn of the century. The United States Environmental Protection Agency has estimated that levels will reach 600 ppm in the next century (between the years 2060 and 2080), which will produce a rise in global air temperature of 1.5–4.5 °C. This appears within the band of temperature rise expected by most authorities, but there are some who expect higher increases and others who expect negligible ones.

1.11   Other greenhouse gases

Carbon dioxide is not the only greenhouse gas; methane, dinitrogen oxide, ozone and chlorofluorocarbons (CFCs) act in a similar way. These are more effective greenhouse gases than carbon dioxide: a molecule of methane is equivalent to 20 molecules of carbon dioxide; and a dinitrogen oxide molecule is equivalent to 200 in this respect. All of these gases are being released to the atmosphere in increasing quantities as a result of the anthropogenic influences.

Methane is a common product of the breakdown of organic matter, including wastes, in anaerobic conditions. There is evidence that it is even produced during the burning of biomass as a result of incomplete oxidation. Methane is released naturally by decomposition in anaerobic estuarine muds, peat bogs and other wetlands but is also produced in increasing volumes from rice paddies, the rumen of cattle, rubbish tips and the burning of forests. Methane in bubbles in ice captured in 1771 is recorded at a level of 0.78 ppm, but by the 1980s this had risen to 1.7 ppm and is increasing at a rate of 1.2% per year.

Dinitrogen oxide and ozone have been mentioned earlier in this chapter. Dinitrogen oxide levels are 0.3 ppm (1991) but expected to rise to 0.35 ppm by the year 2050. Dinitrogen oxide is derived mainly from denitrifying bacteria in the soil which produce dinitrogen oxide from nitrates in the soil under anaerobic conditions. Its increasing concentration is almost certainly due to the escalating use of nitrate fertilisers. Ozone and CFC levels in the atmosphere are also increasing. As well as causing problems by its absence from the stratosphere in polar regions, ozone also enhances global warming through its increasing concentrations in the troposphere.

1.12   Consequences of global warming

The impact of the global warming that has occurred so far is not well known. It has been shown that the density of stomata in plant species has increased by about 40% in the last 200 years in response, it is thought, to the carbon dioxide levels. Increases in growth rates of subalpine conifers in western North America have been recorded and attributed to global warming, as has the decline in red spruce (*Picea rubens*) populations in the USA, but the evidence is not unequivocal. Predictions of future repercussions are not certain, despite global atmospheric models becoming increasingly refined. A particular focus in the debate is the amount of cloud cover predicted by the models. Cloud cover, it is thought, has an impact on incoming solar radiation (cooling) rather greater than its radiation-capturing effect (warming). The complex predictions from the models are difficult to assess, as can be gathered from reading the literature (e.g. Wyman (1991)). There is a consensus, however, that temperature will continue to rise, that parts of the world will become drier and others wetter (see figure 1.10) and that the

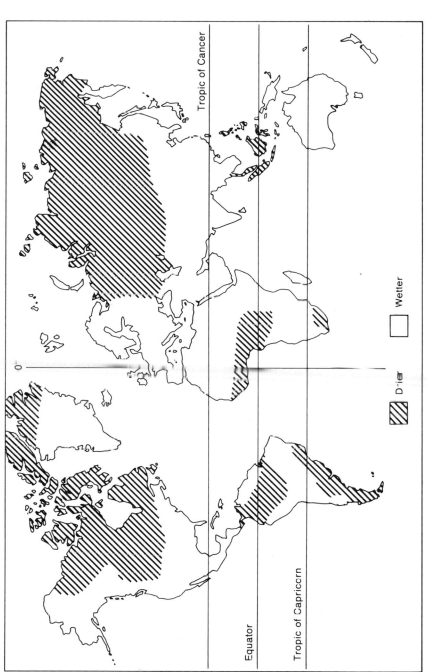

Figure 1.10 A warmer Earth: one prediction for wetter and drier soil moisture patterns in the growing seasons. (Redrawn from Kellogg W. W. & Schware R. (1981) *Climatic change and society,* Westview Press.)

warming will be greater at the poles than at the equator. The change in moisture regimes around the world would lead to significant changes in vegetation and crop growth. The major concern is that areas where rainfall is marginal for agriculture now may become even less productive. It has been suggested that for the UK, by the year 2030, there will be lower rainfall in summer and more in winter in the south east, and higher rainfall in summer and winter in the north and west. Low summer rainfall and increased evapotranspiration may lead to droughts in the south east. The elevated temperatures may make the climate warm enough to grow soya beans and navy beans and to plant sunflowers and maize further north. The range of plants like these is likely to move 300 km north for each degree the temperature rises.

A major effect of global warming will be the melting of polar ice caps and the raising of sea levels. In the last 100 years temperatures have risen about 1 °C and sea levels about 10 cm. Projections of a further increase in sea levels vary between 0.3 m and 3.5 m by the year 2100. This will flood low-lying coastal areas, cause erosion, lead to saltwater intrusion and increase storm damage. Wetland areas will be altered and, as efforts will be made to protect low-lying productive land with polders, it is possible that salt marshes and swamps will disappear by submersion and not be replaced.

1.13 Solutions to problems caused by greenhouse gases

Global warming, as its name implies, is a global and, therefore, international problem which will either be addressed internationally, presumably led by financially prosperous countries through the United Nations, or in practical terms it will be ignored. The solutions are obvious: we have to stop cutting down forests; reduce our burning of fossil fuels; reduce our utilisation of nitrate fertilisers; stop using CFCs and producing other greenhouse gases; and be more careful with our resources. It has been suggested that the resolution of this problem could be achieved by substituting non-renewable fossil fuels with sustainably managed wood fuels (see chapter 4).

The demands for resources and increasing food production, and the wastes produced by these demands, so dominate global biogeochemical cycles and their rate of turnover that their undesirable consequences are being felt on a global scale. Surely it is not possible for over one-third of global nitrogen to be fixed industrially without causing major disruptions to ecosystems that have taken millennia to evolve? Ultimately it is the growing demands placed on resources by an increasing world population that is the source of the problem. This requires the carrying capacity of the globe to be continually raised. It might be a much better idea to seek population stability, or even decline, so that resource demands placed on our environment were sustainable and environmentally friendly in all respects.

1.14   The way forward

Hopes exist for solving global problems. The United Nations has established an Environment Programme (UNEP) to focus world attention on its problems and to make recommendations for their solution. UNEP evolved from the United Nations Conference on the Human Environment in 1972. It has numerous offshoots and subcommittees, for example:

Global Environment Monitoring Systems (GEMS)
INFOTERRA – a scheme for Information Exchange on National Environmental Information
Co-ordinating Committee on the Ozone Layer (CCOL)
The Vienna Ozone Convention

It is hoped that the impacts of global environmental issues will, as a result of this international focus, be fully appreciated and that solutions will be found and implemented to resolve them. Sweden has set an example by placing a carbon dioxide tax on fuels, specifically to cut down greenhouse gas emissions.

An apt conclusion to this chapter is the following extract (about global warming):

Education holds our hope for the future. Environmental education should be the backbone of a new global morality. Every student on the Earth should learn to recognise the finite limits of our planet, that we have the ability to alter its climate and destroy its life-support system. We must come to realise that our future can be made brighter only by limiting our family size and by carefully planned conservative use of natural resources.

Wyman R. L. *et al.* Now what do we do? In Wyman R. L. (ed.) (1991)

Environmental concerns having local impacts

2.1 Eutrophication of freshwater habitats

Freshwater ecosystems have been classified according to the status of nutrients in their waters. Waters that are nutrient-poor and unproductive are **oligotrophic** (Greek *oligos* = few; *trophe* = food). Waters that are rich and, consequently, biologically productive are called **eutrophic** (Greek *eu* = well). Waters which fall somewhere in between are **mesotrophic** (Greek *mesos* = intermediate or middle). The biological productivity of most temperate region freshwaters depends mainly on the level of soluble phosphates and nitrates in the water. Representative data on the level of nutrients and biological productivity in the three classes of temperate lakes are shown in table 2.1.

2.2 Factors which influence the rate of eutrophication

The nutrient status and biological productivity of lakes depend on a number of factors, some of which relate to natural features of a lake's catchment (**natural eutrophication**) and others which are determined largely by the

Table 2.1. Productivity, phytoplankton biomass and the level of phosphorus and inorganic nitrogen in three types of freshwater lakes

Biological and nutrient productivity	Freshwater lake types		
	Oligotrophic	Mesotrophic	Eutrophic
Net primary productivity (g dry weight m^{-2} yr^{-1})	15–50	50–150	150–500
Phytoplankton biomass (mg dry weight m^{-3})	20–200	200–600	600–1000
Total phosphorus (ppb)	< 1–5	5–10	10–30
Inorganic nitrogen (ppb)	< 1–200	200–400	300–650

ppb = parts per billion

Source: Likens G. E. 1975 Primary productivity of inland aquatic systems. In Leith H. & Whittaker R. H. (eds.) *Primary productivity of the biosphere*, Springer-Verlag.

Table 2.2. Nutrient levels in waters from contrasting catchments

Nutrients	Nutrient concentrations (mg dm^{-3})	
	Crummock Water	*River Yare*
Ca	2.1	128.0
Mg	0.8	11.0
Na	3.7	46.0
K	0.3	9.4
HCO$_3$	2.9	238.0
Cl	6.8	77.0

Crummock Water is an oligotrophic lake in the Lake District, on Skiddaw slates (insoluble metamorphic rocks). The River Yare is a eutrophic river which runs into the southern part of the Norfolk Broads, draining the chalk of the Norfolk Edge and running through soft sedimentary rocks and alluvium. In neither of these waters is phosphorus or nitrogen naturally high, although they are now relatively high in the River Yare as a result of pollution.

Source: selected from Macan T. T. 1970 *Biological studies of the English Lakes*, American Elsevier; Moss B. 1983. The Norfolk Broadlands: experiments in the restoration of a complex wetland, *Biological Reviews* **58**:521–61.

anthropogenic influences (**cultural eutrophication**). The most important factors in temperate lakes are:

1 *Fertility of drainage basin*
The natural fertility of a lake basin depends on the rate of weathering of the minerals in the catchment area and the subsequent input of nutrients into its waters (see table 2.2).

2 *Seasonal behaviour of water*
Stagnation caused by the inhibition of the circulation of water by winter ice or the development of a thermocline (thermal stratification) in summer may lead to anaerobic conditions which encourage the release of nutrients, particularly phosphorus, from sediments (see figure 2.1). The anaerobic conditions will also have undesirable influences on aquatic life in the lakes apart from the obvious effects of de-oxygenation; high concentrations of iron (Fe), ammonium ions (NH_4^+) and hydrogen sulphide (H_2S) released from sediments may be toxic to freshwater organisms.

3 *Depth of lake*
Generally, shallow lakes have higher nutrient concentrations than deep lakes and a greater proportion of their volume is shallow enough to allow light to penetrate and support photosynthesis. If lake edges are steep, the most productive margins of deep lakes will be small relative to their volume. Thus shallow lakes tend to be more productive than deep ones.

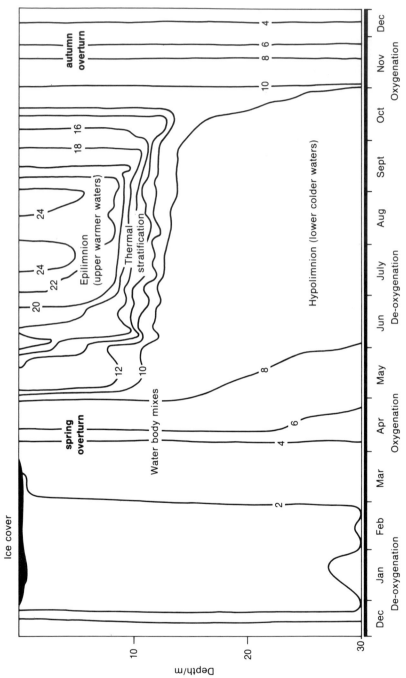

Figure 2.1 Water temperatures in Gull Lake, Michigan, showing the seasonal movement of water body and alternating anaerobic and oxygenated conditions. (Data from Moss B. (1972) in *Freshwater Biology* **2**:289–307.)

4 *Temperature of water*
The warmer the climate, the greater the productivity, all other factors being equal.

5 *Rate of turnover of water*
If water has a short residence time in the lake's body water, opportunities for the nutrients to be captured by biological productivity and incorporated into sediments (i.e. captured in the lake's permanent nutrient capital pool) will be limited.

6 *Cultural eutrophication*
The input of nutrients as a result of human activities in the catchment area.

2.3   Cultural eutrophication of lakes and rivers

The quality of lakes and rivers has caused widespread concern because of a variety of problems:

1 acidification of lake water associated with the acid rain phenomenon, resulting in clear water and the absence of biological productivity (see chapter 1);
2 the introduction of toxic wastes into lakes and rivers; and
3 eutrophication, which produces an excess of undesirable biological productivity.

The objective of many activities is to increase biological productivity in managed ecosystems. Nutrients (fertilisers) are deliberately added to the soil in agriculture, horticulture and forestry to increase yield and profitability. The same process is used in some parts of the world to increase the productivity of freshwater ponds to provide high harvests of fish. Sewage is allowed to flow into highly eutrophic ponds to fertilise the growth of algae which are then consumed by fish, a valuable source of protein in many Third World countries. In this situation eutrophication can only be seen as desirable!

The undesirable features of excessive biological productivity, often associated with cultural eutrophication, can be seen from this list of the properties of highly eutrophic (**hypereutrophic**) waters:

1 The water is turbid. Light penetration in severe conditions may be limited to a few centimetres below the surface.
2 There is a lack of species-richness of the fauna and flora in the water. Very highly enriched waters may be dominated by the sewage fungus (*Sphaerotilus natans* – actually a filamentous bacterium). Macroscopic animals may be restricted to one or two species of tubificid worms.

3 The variety of fish life is changed from the species characteristic of well-oxygenated, clear waters (e.g. char (*Salvelinus* spp.), trout (*Salmo trutta*) and whitefish (a variety of species of the family Coregonidae)) to those species which will tolerate low-oxygen conditions (e.g. roach (*Rutilus rutilus*), bream (*Abramis brama*) and carp (*Cyprinus carpio*)).

4 In eutrophic conditions there may be a switch from aerobic decomposition processes, which release carbon dioxide, water and oxidised sulphur compounds (ultimately sulphate ions (SO_4^{2-})), to anaerobic decomposition, which produces methane (CH_4) and hydrogen sulphide (H_2S) gases.

The effects of eutrophication, as suggested by C. F. Mason (1981), cause further problems:

1 Treatment of the water for drinking may be difficult.
2 Growth of algae may leave unacceptable tastes or odours in water supplies.
3 The water may be injurious to health.
4 The amenity value is reduced.
5 Growth of plants may inhibit water flow and navigation.
6 The loss of salmonids and coregonids from the water may have economic consequences for fisheries.

2.4   Causes of cultural eutrophication

Freshwater productivity is most often limited by the level of soluble phosphate and nitrate in the water. It is necessary, therefore, to examine human activities which cause the level of these nutrients to increase in water. Nitrate is readily soluble and is easily leached from soil. Phosphate, on the other hand, is fixed by most soils, usually combining with calcium to form insoluble calcium phosphate ($Ca_3(PO_4)_2$). Phosphate is usually only lost from soil when there is erosion of soil particles, which may contain substantial quantities of insoluble (and hence unavailable) phosphate. Terrestrial habitats tend not to leak substantial quantities of soluble phosphate into water courses under normal circumstances. Soil erosion may increase phosphate levels in water, but this is not necessarily available for biological productivity unless it is taken into solution.

The modifications to the natural pathways by which these compounds reach water is well shown by studies on the sources of nutrients in the catchment of Lake Wisconsin, USA, a lake that was becoming increasingly eutrophic. The data are summarised in table 2.3. The largest source of nitrate is from rural groundwater and is believed to have arrived there as a direct or indirect effect of inorganic fertiliser nitrate leaching from the soil. A second major source of nitrate is derived from sewage treatment facilities, but it is

Table 2.3. Percentage of nitrogen and phosphorus entering Lake Wisconsin surface waters from different parts of the catchment area

Source	Nitrogen	Phosphorus
*Municipal treatment facilities**	31.2	58.7
Urban run-off	5.5	10.0
Rural sources		
Manured land	9.9	21.5
Other cropland	0.7	3.1
Forest land	0.5	0.3
Pasture, woodland, etc.	0.7	2.9
Rural groundwater	42.0	2.3
Precipitation on water areas	8.5	1.2

* Includes a small input from private sewage systems and industrial wastes.
Source: Hassler A. D. 1974. Cultural eutrophication is reversible. In Cox G. W. (ed.) *Readings in conservation ecology,* Prentice Hall. (Originally appeared in *Bioscience* (1969) **19(5)**: 425–431.)

these which supply by far the largest proportion of the phosphate reaching the lake. The only other large phosphate source is manured land, where the nutrients are derived from animal waste.

The ultimate sources of these nutrients in Lake Wisconsin and most other lakes are, obviously, agricultural practices and sewage effluent.

2.5 Agricultural practices leading to eutrophication

On a global scale, the amount of nitrogen fixed from the atmosphere by the Haber process is over one-third the amount fixed by natural processes. Most of this is used in the manufacture of fertilisers for increasing agricultural productivity. The use of nitrogenous fertilisers has increased dramatically in the twentieth century (see figure 2.2). In parallel, an increase in nitrate levels has been recorded in many water bodies (see figure 2.3). The nitrate-in-water story is not, however, just a simple one of excess nitrate fertiliser leaching from the soil. Work at Rothamsted Experimental Station, Hertfordshire, indicates that most applied nitrogen fertiliser is tied up in organic material and leaching occurs when this material is decomposed and the nitrate is remineralised. Decomposition is fastest in soil in the autumn when the soil is still warm and becoming moist enough to provide good conditions for microbial activity. The nitrate is vulnerable to leaching when crop cover and growth (and hence crop uptake of nitrogen) is low and there is sufficient rainfall to remove the available nitrogen. Any farming operation which

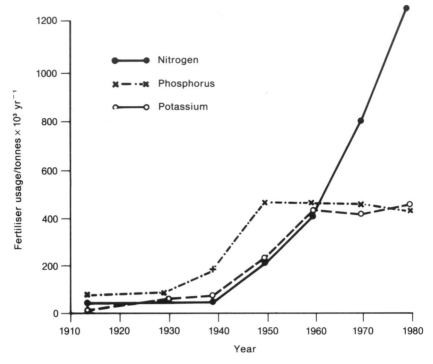

Figure 2.2 The use of fertilisers in the UK during part of the twentieth century. (Data from Briggs & Courtney (1989).)

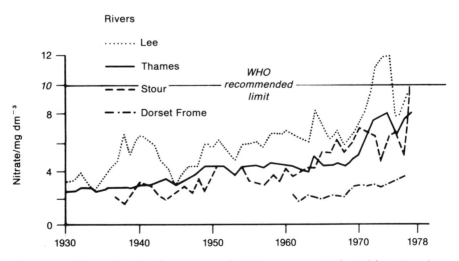

Figure 2.3 Nitrate levels in four rivers in the UK since 1930. (Adapted from Royal Society Study Group (1983) *The nitrogen cycle of the United Kingdom*, The Royal Society.)

introduces large quantities of organic material into the soil will also lead to leaching of nitrates, particularly at times of high rainfall, and when there is no actively growing crop. This happens at the time grassland is ploughed for arable cropping. The nitrogen capital built up in the organic part of the soil and in the plants will be released quickly as decomposition proceeds, and if there is no growing crop to take up the released nitrate it will be leached by rain percolating through the soil. It takes decades for water to percolate from the surface to the groundwater. It is believed that the high nitrate levels found in groundwater in East Anglia (1990s) are derived from the ploughing-up of grassland and changes in agricultural practices at the end of the Second World War (1945).

Whatever the mechanism involved, there is little doubt that the nitrates causing eutrophication in waters are mainly derived, directly or indirectly, from changing farming practices and increasing fertiliser utilisation. In the UK, knowledge of crop nutrient uptake, nutrient behaviour in soil and farming practice has enabled the Rothamsted scientist, T. Addiscott to recommend a code of good farming practice for the use of nitrate fertilisers:

- Do not apply nitrogen fertiliser in autumn.
- Do not leave the soil bare in winter.
- Sow winter crops early in autumn.
- If a spring crop is to be sown, grow a winter catch crop.
- Use animal manures judiciously.
- Do not plough up too large a proportion of grassland in any one area at any particular time.
- Plough in straw. This locks up some nitrate in organic matter but may lead to increased nitrate production in the long term.
- Use nitrogen fertiliser strictly in accordance with professional advice. Apply it only when the crop is growing actively.

2.6   Sewage effluent and cultural eutrophication

If agricultural practices have been mainly responsible for the nitrates that have caused eutrophication in rivers and lakes, it is clear that sewage effluent has also contributed an additional nitrate load (see table 2.3). It is the contribution of sewage effluent to the phosphate loadings that has ensured that both of these rate-limiting nutrients are in abundant supply for high biological productivity in waters. Animal wastes, including human wastes, contain significant quantities of soluble phosphorus, but the largest input of phosphate from domestic sources is from detergents, which were first introduced on a large scale for domestic washing purposes in the early 1950s. Normal detergents contain 5–12% by weight phosphorus and may contribute up to half the phosphate load on sewage treatment facilities. The impact of the effluent from a sewage treatment works on the phosphate

Table 2.4. Total phosphorus concentrations from lake sediments

Date	Phosphorus concentration ($\mu g\ dm^{-3}$)	Significant action
1800	13	
1900	52	
1920	72	
1924	—	Sewage treatment works constructed
1940	119	
early 1950s	—	Phosphate detergents introduced
1974–6	361	

Source: O'Riordan T. 1979. Alarm calls for the Broads: signs of disaster and a policy for survival, *Geographical Magazine* **L11(1)**:50–56.

levels of Barton Broad, East Anglia, was demonstrated in data derived from its sediments (see table 2.4).

2.7 Solution of problems caused by eutrophication

The biological productivity of eutrophic rivers and lakes can be reduced by decreasing the inflow of one of the rate-limiting nutrients, nitrate or soluble phosphate, into the water. Nitrogen is not easily controlled; it is readily soluble and widely available in waters as a result of agricultural practices. In the presence of adequate phosphorus but with an absence of nitrates in water, it is possible for some forms of aquatic micro-organisms, such as the cyanobacteria (blue-green bacteria), to fix atmospheric nitrogen. The best option for solving problems of eutrophication is to reduce phosphate levels, especially as it is cheaper to remove phosphorus than nitrogen at sewage treatment plants.

Phosphate levels in sewage effluent can be reduced in several ways. One is to use detergents with a very low phosphorus content. However, models of phosphate behaviour in water suggest that this technique is not likely to be sufficient on its own. A further method is the tertiary treatment of effluent from the sewage treatment process (phosphorus stripping). High efficiencies, up to 95% phosphate removal, can be achieved by precipitation of the phosphorus using chemicals such as lime (calcium carbonate $CaCO_3$) or ammonium iron(III) sulphate (($NH_4)_2SO_4.Fe_2(SO_4)_3.24H_2O$). This process has not always been as successful as expected in many attempts at reducing the trophic status of lakes. It has often been found that a substantial capital of phosphate has built up in the sediments of such lakes, from which the water body can replenish its phosphate. Replenishment occurs readily if the lake bottom sediments become anaerobic and phosphates are released from organic colloids. To achieve successful control of eutrophication under these circumstances it may be necessary to remove the sediment; this has been done in Lake Trummen, southern Sweden. Removal of sediment and diversion of polluted waste water from the lake has resulted in a marked improvement in its condition, where diversion in itself proved inadequate because of the phosphate capital in the sediments.

2.8 Oil spills

Oil pollution of the oceans is a significant environmental concern, but one which appears, since the 1970s, to be gradually declining in global terms, except for losses from tankers at sea. Discharges from shipping, losses from coastal refineries and offshore production losses have remained more or less constant or have reduced over this period. Only about 6% of the oil in oceans is derived from natural sources (see table 2.5).

Oil entering the sea from shipping disasters is an important but, over a period of time, a relatively small part of total oil pollution. Environmental damage results from all oil spills, but is particularly dramatic with large disasters and if moderate spills occur in the 'wrong' place. Amongst the more dramatic oil spill incidents have been the *Torrey Canyon* in 1967 (117 000 tonnes of oil lost) and the *Amoco Cadiz* in 1978 (230 000 tonnes) (both in the English Channel), the *Exxon Valdes* in 1989 in Prince William Sound off the Alaskan coast and, the largest oil spill ever, the *IXTOC 1* oil platform blowout in the Gulf of Mexico (400 000 tonnes). The massive loss of oil on

Table 2.5. Estimates of sources of petroleum hydrocarbons in the oceans

Sources	Estimated rates (10^3 MT year^{-1})
Natural seepages	200
Atmospheric deposition	300
Urban run-off and discharges	1080
Coastal refineries	100
Other coastal effluent	50
Accidents from tankers at sea	400
Operational discharges from tankers	700
Losses from other shipping	320
Offshore production losses	50
Total	3200

MT = million tonnes

Source: Koons B. B. 1984. Input of petroleum to the marine environment, *Marine Technology Society Journal* **18**:97–112.

land and at sea following the Gulf War (1991) has yet to be quantified. Each separate oil spill is a unique event whose consequences depend on: the nature of the petroleum hydrocarbon (oil cargoes vary widely); the toxicity to different types of marine life of the particular oil; wind and other weather conditions; and the habitat on which the oil is spilled. Following a spill the oil undergoes a series of transformations:

1 It spreads on the surface and light fractions evaporate, leaving denser oils, which may sink.
2 Some of the components of oil are soluble.
3 Rough weather breaks up the slick and incorporates small droplets of oil into water as an emulsion.
4 Material remaining on the surface is thoroughly mixed and emulsified with water to form mousse (so named because of its consistency). Mousse is the material that most often reaches the shore.
5 Following oxidation reactions involving biological material and bright light, the surface oil is broken down to form asphaltic tar balls, which may persist for some time on or in the water body.

Petroleum hydrocarbons are toxic, although the water-soluble ones are less so. The oil at sea kills sea birds and plankton – the latter may rapidly return to normal numbers after oil has disappeared. The severest effects appear to be caused when the mousse is washed ashore. When the *Amoco Cadiz* went aground off the coast of Brittany, north west France, about a third of the spilled oil washed ashore on beaches and rocks. Detergents and oil dispersants were used only in restricted areas and were selected for their low toxicity to marine organisms (detergents that had been used in earlier clean-up operations often caused as much death of marine life as the oil itself). Most of the oil was removed by shovelling up contaminated sand and tarry residues. The pollution was, typically, much longer lasting in estuaries than on beaches or rocky shores and was still causing concern six years later. It damaged the estuarine oyster (*Ostrea edulis*) fisheries by tainting the oysters' flesh, although the animals appeared not to be affected. Invertebrates on the beaches were more heavily affected than those of the rocky shore and in some areas the normal beach community became dominated by large numbers of one or two oil-tolerant species. Seaweeds were severely damaged by direct contact with the oil, but gradually recovered. Salt marsh vegetation and eelgrass (*Zostera marina*) recovered quickly because shoots in the mud were not killed and they resprouted after the oil had been removed.

Following the *Torrey Canyon* disaster efforts have been made to improve methods for clean-up after spills. Less toxic oil dispersants and detergents have been developed. Chemicals, booms, pumps, bulldozers, small oil tanks and other equipment are kept at strategic points to be available should further spills occur. Contingency plans and, for some areas, maps of sensitivity to oils spills have been developed. The maps show the likely length of time a spill would persist (an oil residency index) and the degree and persistence of damage to ecosystems (a biological sensitivity index). Such maps would assist the determination of priorities for protection from spilled oil and for a programme for clean-up operations. Following the recognition of the effectiveness of microbial activity in clearing up oil spills on land in temperate and tropical regions, research is being undertaken on this as a method for dealing with coastal oil damage.

Oil spills on land are easier to deal with because they are not likely to be large in extent and are not dispersed. Even in arctic conditions many plants will recover after exposure to oil and will re-invade damaged areas. The difficulty in cold conditions is that the very low temperatures make recovery very slow, although this can be assisted by introducing arctic grasses and using fertilisers. A beneficial spin-off from oil exploration in arctic regions has been the increase in our knowledge of tundra ecosystems. Many scientists are convinced that the environmental problems resulting from the development of arctic oilfields are much more likely to be derived from the problems of urbanisation and transport than from oils spills.

2.9 Atmospheric pollution

This topic is covered in chapter 1 from the perspective of global atmospheric pollution, but there are three significant areas where atmospheric pollution has an impact at local levels. These are photochemical smog, carbon monoxide and lead contamination from tetraethyl lead, all of which are closely related to pollution caused by the internal combustion engine.

2.10 Photochemical smog

Photochemical smogs (photochemical oxidants) are caused by the action of bright sunlight on a mixture of reactive hydrocarbons and oxides of nitrogen from vehicle exhausts. The most important products of the reactions are ozone and peroxyacetyl nitrate (PAN). The significance of ozone as a greenhouse gas and as an atmospheric filter for UV radiation has been described in chapter 1. Both ozone and PAN are significant in their effect on human health and plant life. They cause headaches and eye irritation and, at higher concentrations, coughs and chest discomfort. Although rarely responsible for causing mortality, evidence suggests that they may be for old people when combined with high temperatures. The long-term effects of exposure to photochemical oxidants are not known.

Photochemical smog causes damage to materials, for example rubber, paints and textiles, at quite low concentrations. It is also toxic to plants, causing necrotic patches or chlorosis on foliage. A number of plants are known to be particularly sensitive, for example spinach, tomatoes and tobacco. Sensitive strains of tobacco have been used to monitor this type of pollution as there is a high correlation between severity of damage symptoms and ozone concentration. Forests of ponderosa pine (*Pinus ponderosa*) have been severely affected in California and many authorities believe that ozone is playing an important role in forest decline in Europe.

The phenomenon was first recognised in Los Angeles, California, where the concentration of these gases can rise to very high levels because of two important factors:

1 the very high density of motor traffic;
2 the climate and topography of California, which cause temperature inversions and trap air in the steep-sided valleys.

Photochemical smogs occur in many areas and have become prominent since the 1970s; they have also been recorded in Sydney, Tokyo, central Europe and London. In London the episodes (not to be confused with the sulphurous coal-derived smogs of the 1950s and 1960s) are associated with slow moving anti-cyclonic air masses which drift into southern England, collecting ozone from atmospheric pollution in central Europe.

A variety of acceptable atmospheric ozone limits have been set in different parts of the world, with the objectives of reducing impacts on either plants or human comfort. In the USA a maximum one-hour concentration of 120 parts per billion (ppb) once a year is the legal limit, Sweden has a guideline value of 60 ppb maximum one-hour concentration, and WHO (World Health Organisation) recommends a maximum level of 60 ppb maximum one-hour concentration for preventing significant plant damage. Even at these levels crop productivity would be reduced by a factor of 2–4%. WHO have recommended levels of 60 ppb maximum one-hour concentration, or 30 ppb maximum eight-hour concentration, for the long-term protection of public health. It is noted, however, that headaches will appear at concentrations of 50 ppb for one hour and eye irritation at 150 ppb.

2.11 Carbon monoxide

The volume of carbon monoxide (CO) produced from the incomplete oxidation of fuels and released from industrial processes is slightly greater than that derived from natural sources. This gas is a health hazard because it is absorbed by the lungs and combines more or less irreversibly with haemoglobin in the blood to form **carboxyhaemoglobin**. This compound is also produced as a result of inhaling tobacco smoke. People exposed to high levels of carbon monoxide over long periods (e.g. petrol pump and parking lot attendants, traffic policemen and vehicle drivers) may have carboxy-haemoglobin levels in excess of 2% in the blood – the approximate threshold level at which undesirable symptoms appear. At blood levels of 2–10% the symptoms are of tiredness, impaired vigilance and loss of manual dexterity.

Beyond this, symptoms become increasingly serious: at 30–40% they are incapacitating; at 60–70% coma is likely; and above 70% death ensues. All this can happen without the victim being aware of the cause of distress, as carbon monoxide is a colourless, odourless, non-irritating gas. Prolonged exposure has been associated with defective heart valves. WHO recommended carboxyhaemoglobin levels in blood should be maintained below 3%, which means that exposure to carbon monoxide should not be over 50 ppm in 30 minutes, 25 ppm over 1 hour and 10 ppm over 8–24 hours.

2.12   Lead derived from anti-knock petrol

Tetraethyl ($Pb(CH_2CH_3)_4$) and tetramethyl ($Pb(CH_3)_4$) lead have been added to petrol since 1923 to increase the efficiency of car engines and to prolong engine life by reducing knock. Knocking is a premature explosion of fuel due to overcompression. The end product of this use is the release of lead into the atmosphere in association with very small particulate matter. It is found in high concentrations in the atmosphere near roads and accumulates in soil and on surfaces. Most of the lead produced settles within 50 m of roads, but about a third is transported over greater distances. Lead concentrations in polar ice samples have increased and 90% of that found in recent ice has been attributed to anthropogenic sources.

Abnormally high levels of lead absorbed from the air or ingested cause a variety of symptoms in humans. The digestion of lead-contaminated dust, which may originate from vehicle exhausts, lead-based paints and smelters, is an important route into the body. Lead is not readily eliminated as it binds irreversibly to proteins and accumulates in the body. Lead has been implicated in anaemia, hypertension, hyperactivity and brain damage. Even low levels of lead, which do not produce classical symptoms of lead poisoning, have been linked to behavioural and learning difficulties in inner-city school children. It is also toxic to plants, and verges of very busy roads may be devoid of vegetation or their plant communities highly modified as lead-sensitive species are eliminated.

The use of lead-free paints has been encouraged since the 1950s, but it has taken society a long time to address the problem of vehicle-emitted lead. This has now been addressed by, for example, the use of lead-free petrol promoted by government publicity and small discounts in fuel prices. This change has been introduced because of two environmental concerns:

1 the need to reduce environmental lead concentrations;
2 to prevent poisoning of catalytic converters in cars, which are designed to reduce the production of carbon monoxide, unburned hydrocarbons and oxides of nitrogen.

As a result atmospheric lead concentrations in the UK have fallen since the widespread introduction of lead-free petrol in the late 1980s.

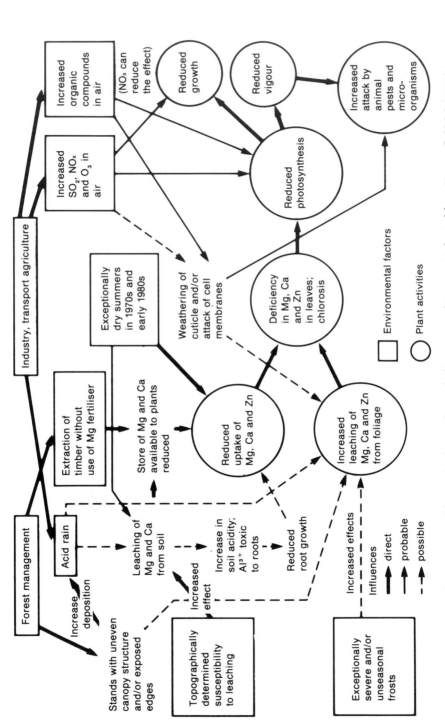

Figure 2.4 Interaction of environmental factors leading to forest decline in central Europe. (Adapted from Krause G.H.M. (1989) in Grubb P.J. & Whittaker J.B. *Toward a more exact ecology*, Blackwell Scientific.)

2.13   Forest decline in Europe

The problem of a **novel forest decline** in France, Germany, Switzerland, Austria and northern Italy was first reported in the 1980s. The cause of the decline has been the subject of considerable argument, almost certainly as a result of the complexity and inter-relationships of causative factors. One interpretation of this complex situation (see figure 2.4) shows how some pollutants (see chapters 1 and 2) can interact. This major environmental problem arises from the interplay between:

1 forest management
2 the impact of pollutants derived from agriculture, industry and transport
3 unusual climatic events (drought and frost)
4 topography
5 pests and diseases.

Land-use changes and their consequences to ecosystems

3.1 Agricultural change

The pressures on the environment resulting from agricultural changes have received much attention. Major changes in agricultural activity since the 1940s in the UK include:

1 *Increasing levels of farm mechanisation, energy inputs and decline in the labour force*
This long-term change accelerated after the Second World War.

2 *Development of highly productive strains of crops and livestock*
For example, as a result of genetic improvements, spring barley yields have increased by an average of 0.84% per year in the last 30 years.

3 *Increasing use of fertilisers and pesticides*
Fertiliser use has increased about 8 times in the last 50 years, with nitrate application showing the greatest increase at about 16 times. Coupled with the development of highly productive strains of crops, there has been a marked rise in crop productivity. Agricultural food production in the UK has increased by a factor of about 100% since 1955, for example yields per hectare of wheat and barley have nearly doubled, root crop production has increased by 50–75% and milk volumes per cow have increased by about 50%.

4 *Changes in farm size*
Between 1949 and 1979 the number of farms which were larger than 122 ha in the UK increased from 12 317 to 16 765. Accompanying this has been an increase in field sizes to accommodate larger machinery and reduce the proportion of non-productive headlands used for turning. The removal of hedgerows, as a consequence, has been substantial (see below).

5 *Changes in farming practices and significance of different crops*
The most significant change in the crops grown in the UK has been a decline in the area of grassland and an increase in arable crops. Sugar

Table 3.1. Changes in area of agricultural crops in the UK

Crop	% of total area used for agriculture			
	1938	*1979*	*1985*	*1990*
Wheat	4.2	7.5	10.8	10.9
Barley	2.2	12.8	8.1	8.2
Oats	4.6	0.9	0.6	0.6
Potatoes	1.3	1.1	0.9	1.0
Sugar beet	0.7	1.2	1.0	1.0
Turnips and swedes	1.6	—	—	—
Mangolds	0.5	—	—	—
Oilseed rape	0.0	0.4	2.1	2.1
Temporary grass	7.5	10.0	8.4	8.5
Permanent grass	38.4	27.9	28.1	28.4
Total area (million ha)	18.36	18.36	18.70	18.51

Permanent grass is 5 years or older, temporary grass is under 5 years. Most of the area unaccounted for in this table is rough grazing.
Source: Nix (1991); Briggs & Courtney (1989).

beet, beans, peas and oilseeds (oilseed rape first and later linseed) are arable crops that have increased in area, while oats, rye and turnips have declined. The increase in arable farming has also had an influence on hedgerow removal – arable crops do not have to be kept in the fields! The increase in the sugar beet area has also had an impact outside the UK, causing hardship for tropical sugar producers who grow sugar cane, not sugar beet. They have seen exports dwindle and their overseas earnings decline. Some of the changes in the total agricultural land area used for major crops are shown in table 3.1.

6 *Financial returns*

In real terms financial returns to farmers remained relatively stable from 1940 to about 1977, with an exceptional year of high return in 1973. Since then returns have declined – those for the early 1990s are about 40% of the value for the period 1940–77, yet the Retail Price Index more or less doubled between 1980 and 1990.

The effect of these developments on wildlife values are summarised in figure 3.1, which provides a suitable model to bear in mind when considering the issues raised in this chapter.

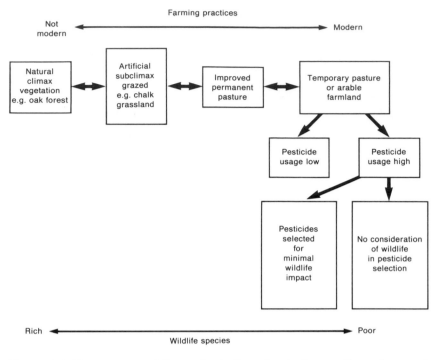

Figure 3.1 Consequences of the modernisation of agriculture on the ecology and wildlife interests of farmland. (Adapted from Briggs D. J. & Courtney F. M. (1989).)

3.2   Influence of the EC on agricultural change

Some of the changes in cropping in the UK came partly as a result of the CAP (Common Agriculture Policy) and EC (European Community) subsidies. The changing pattern of agricultural subsidy from the EC has resulted in changes in crops grown. The subsidy for oilseeds, introduced to raise EC prices and production, has generated bright yellow patches of oilseed rape in parts of the countryside, to which the subtle shades of blue linseed are now being added. Farm production within the EC is often protected by import levies or quotas, through the CAP. Price and production support and some form of import protection for the EC is given, for example to milk and milk products (although a quota system limits production), beef, sheepmeat, pork, cereals, oilseeds, sugar, and fruit and vegetables. Special arrangements have been made so that certain Third World and, recently, Eastern Bloc countries are not disadvantaged. An international agreement on free world trade, GATT (General Agreement on Tariffs and Trade), has been deadlocked (as at 1992) for six years partly because of disagreements over agricultural subsidies.

Table 3.2. Self-sufficiency in farm products in the UK (selected data)

Plant products	%*	Animal products	%*
Wheat	127	Beef and veal	93
Barley	128	Mutton and lamb	94
Oats	99	Pork	98
Rye/mixed corn	90	Bacon and ham	42
Oilseed rape	98	Poultry	95
Potatoes	89	Butter	65
Sugar	56	Cheese	64
Hops	85	Cream	108
Apples	41	Eggs	93
Pears	24	Wool	80
Cauliflowers	88		
Tomatoes	35		

* Production as percentage of new supply for use in the UK, 1990 estimates.
Source: Nix (1991).

3.3 Overproduction of food in Europe

Overproduction within the EC has led to the development of 'lakes' (wine and milk) and 'mountains' (butter, beef and cereals) of produce held in store. These surpluses have been redistributed to be of considerable help to countries suffering from drought and famine or when political upheaval has resulted in the disruption of farming or food distribution. The surpluses have frequently been criticised, however, generally on the grounds of over-production, though some commentators have pointed out that the grain held in store, for example, would be insufficient to last a year if there was a widescale crop disaster.

The UK has become more and more self-sufficient in producing its own food requirements, though large quantities of food that cannot be produced in a temperate climate are of course imported – bananas, dessert grapes, currants, raisins, sultanas, tea and coffee, oranges and other citrus fruits, navy beans (for processing into baked beans) and rice. Although concerns about overproduction are often voiced, the UK is only 56.4% self-sufficient for *all* food and animal feed, and with indigenous food and animal feed the figure is still only 73.5%. Of the major crops the production of cereals is the only one for which the UK markedly exceeds self sufficiency levels (see table 3.2).

It is the EC as a whole that is producing surpluses (wine, dairy products, beef, cereals). However, future projections for the agricultural industry of the UK suggest that much land could go out of production without compromising current (early 1990s) self-sufficiency levels. It is thought the UK could be 80% self-sufficient in temperate products whilst farming only 77% of the present agricultural land area (leaving about 4.3 million hectares surplus land). According to work by Wye College, if increases in farm productivity continue to the end of the century, the UK would require 3 million hectares *less* land – equivalent to an area the combined size of the counties of Northumberland, Cumbria, Tyne and Wear, Durham, North Yorkshire, Lancashire, Humberside and Cleveland being taken out of agriculture.

3.4 Solutions to overproduction

There are three main ways in which overproduction of food could be reduced, all of which would have important consequences for the quality of the landscape and the environment:

1 Farmers could be urged to become less productive through using fewer inorganic fertilisers. This would reduce not only productivity but also the leaching of soluble components of fertilisers into groundwater and freshwater ecosystems.
2 Some farmland could be converted to woodland.
3 Part of the agricultural land stock of the country could be taken out of intensive production; in other words an agricultural extensification or a set-aside system (in official documents referred to as a reconversion and extensification scheme). This would concentrate high-intensity farming on a smaller proportion of suitable land.

In all three cases it would be possible to target areas where either the impact of fertiliser run-off was known to be severe or woodland or low-intensity farming would enhance landscape quality or conservation interests. Obviously farmers would need to be compensated financially by the government for any losses in production.

3.5 Environmentally Sensitive and Nitrate Sensitive Areas

Following the introduction of the scheme (1987) in five areas, 12 localities in the UK have been designated as Environmentally Sensitive Areas (ESAs). These are areas where the landscape and wildlife are of special importance and where these features are particularly vulnerable to the effects of agricultural intensification. They are the Pennine Dales, North Peak, Lleyn Peninsula, Cambrian Mountains, Shropshire Borders, Breckland, the Broads, Suffolk River Valleys, Somerset Levels and Moors, Test Valley, South Downs and West Penwith. Incentive payments are made to farmers for agreements relating to the management of land, walls, buildings and other features in ways which conserve the landscape that had been created by traditional land-use management.

In a similar manner a number of areas have been designated Nitrate Sensitive Areas (NSAs) with the objective of reducing nitrate levels in water supplies to levels below the EC permitted level (50 mg 1^{-1}). This scheme restricts the use of fertiliser, slurry and manure applications, and encourages the use of nitrate-absorbing cover crops, in order to reduce the levels of nitrate leaching into water supplies.

3.6   Farm woodland

Two schemes have been introduced in the UK to encourage the development of woodland on farms (apart from the set-aside scheme, see below). These are the Woodland Grant Scheme and the Farm Woodland Scheme. The first scheme, administered by the Forestry Commission, provides grants for establishment and management, the grants being slightly more generous for broad-leaved as opposed to coniferous woodlands. The Farm Woodland Scheme is administered by the Ministry of Agriculture Fisheries and Food and was introduced in 1988. It is additional to and dependent on the Woodland Grant Scheme. Its purpose is to assist in supporting the developer between the time of planting the trees and receiving income from thinnings. The UK receives reimbursement for both schemes from the EC. The objectives are to produce timber, enhance the landscape, improve wildlife values, create recreational opportunities and assist farm profitability and rural employment.

3.7   Set-aside

A farming extensification plan was adopted by the EC in a 1988 amendment to the 1985 EC Structures Regulations. This required EC governments to facilitate the extensification of both crop and livestock production. Set-aside is an EC initiative and details of its implementation in the UK are complex. Grants are made to farmers to set-aside at least 20% of their land from arable production. At the same time the scheme ensures that the land set aside is kept in good agricultural condition (this includes its use for woodland) and in a way that is compatible with environmental protection. The land could be used for permanent fallow or woodland (a grant of £222 ha^{-1} in Lowland or £202 ha^{-1} in Less Favoured Areas, 1991 prices), rotational fallow (comparable figures are £202 and £182) or non-agricultural use (£150 and £130). Applications of pesticides and fertilisers are strictly regulated. A more detailed description can be found in Nix (1991).

Some agricultural production is permitted on set-aside land and its management is not without costs. It is a voluntary scheme and the choice of land that is set aside is fortuitous, resulting from an individual's choice rather than what might be considered best from the nation's point of view. Some selectivity is managed by differential payments in two ways:

1 *Differential funding for Lowland and Less Favoured Areas*
This is a reflection on financial returns from the land prior to set-aside, but equally wildlife and landscape have been more seriously affected by intensification in lowland areas.

2 *Premium Scheme administered by Countryside Commission*
Additional funds were made available for farmers in the east of England (Norfolk, Suffolk, Essex, Cambridgeshire, Hertforshire, Bedfordshire and Northamptonshire − counties which have suffered considerably from very intensive arable farming and the removal of woodlands and hedgerows) to improve landscape and wildlife values. The grants were for five distinct purposes: wildlife fallow; wooded field margins; winter grazing for Brent geese (*Branta bernicla*); recreational meadowland; and habitat restoration (e.g. to heathland, wet meadow or chalk grassland).

Many of the schemes described in the sections above are pilot schemes or in early stages of their development. Their full and continuing impact on landscape, wildlife and environmental quality has yet to be seen. It is encouraging that environmental concerns are being addressed, although these are not always the prime reasons for the adoption of the schemes.

3.8 Hedgerow removal

One of the consequences of agricultural intensification, the development and use of large machines, and the economies of scale, has been the increase in size of fields and the reduction in the length of hedgerows (see table 3.3)

Rates of loss of about $8000 \, \text{km yr}^{-1}$ are frequently quoted as average values for the UK, a figure that was estimated for the period between 1945 and 1970. Other advantages of hedgerow removal additional to the features mentioned above, have been identified:

1 Hedgerows act as refuges and/or overwintering sites for weeds, diseases and pests.
2 Hedgerows reduce crop yields adjacent to the hedge, particularly where soil moisture deficits are a problem.

Hedgerows are, however, an important component of the countryside because they are of high landscape and conservation value:

1 They add diversity to and are a traditional feature of the landscape.
2 They provide foraging, roosting and nesting sites for birds.
3 They are rich in animal and plant species. It has been estimated about 500 vascular plant species are found in hedgerows in the UK. Closely

Table 3.3. Rate of removal of hedgerows in eastern England

Date	Rate of removal (km year^{-1})
1946–54	1300
1954–62	3900
1962–66	5600
1966–70	3200

Source: Pollard E. *et al.* 1974 *Hedges*, Collins.

associated with these plants are a host of insects, molluscs, spiders and small animals. Elm trees (*Ulmus* spp.) which occur more frequently in hedges than anywhere else, provide food for about 100 species of insect. It has been suggested that, in many intensive arable areas, woodland and scrub is scarce and hedgerows represent a last refuge for animal populations. It appears that the grasses and herbs at the bottom of the hedge are particularly important because of the high animal and plant species richness found there. Research on a novel form of **field break**, a hedge without the woody plants (if you can call it a hedge!), has clearly demonstrated this and shown that the biological control of pests in adjacent crops is enhanced by its presence. Field breaks act as a source of beneficial insects, which have limited powers of dispersal, allowing such insects to penetrate into all parts of the crop.

4 Hedgerows act as wildlife corridors so that flora and fauna have routes for dispersal from the remnant islands of wildlife habitat through an increasingly hostile agricultural landscape. Hedges not only assist the rather obviously expected movements of birds, large mammals (e.g. foxes (*Vulpes vulpes*) and badgers (*Meles meles*)) and small mammals (e.g. shrews (*Sorex* spp. and *Neomys* spp.), voles (*Clethrionomys* spp. and *Microtus* spp.) and mice (*Apodemus* spp., *Micromys minutus* and *Mus musculus*)), but also the much slower dispersal of other organisms (e.g. ground beetles, molluscs and plants).

3.9 Monoculture

A long-standing feature of agriculture is the utilisation of large areas of crops consisting entirely of one plant species, or even a single plant variety, with a very narrow genetic base. Similarly, animals used in farming are highly selected. There has been much debate about the risks of monocultures. The advantages of using crop monocultures in agriculture (and plantation forestry) are obvious. The species, or strains of species, are selected for the conditions under which they are grown and to provide the highest possible yields. Crop growth, response to fertilisers, as well as flowering and ripening, will occur simultaneously and consistently in any area planted at the same time. A uniform crop will be harvested. The consistent product is readily handled by machinery in the field and in the processing and packaging factories, and is appreciated by the customer.

The concerns about monocultures originate from the view that they are inherently unstable and that crops with a narrow genetic base are particularly vulnerable to pests and diseases. This position is derived from the widely accepted (but not incontrovertibly established) belief that the stability of plant and animal communities is positively related to their diversity. The corollary of this belief is that monocultures – communities with minimal diversity – are unstable. Described in simple ecological terms, complex (diverse) ecosystems have many interacting and interrelated components with complex food webs, whereas simple (monocultural) ecosystems have few interacting links and possess linear food chains (see figure 3.2). Disruption of one or a few of the interactions in a complex ecosystem will leave sufficient links, thus maintaining the overall stability of the ecosystem. With a linear food chain, removal of a single link will probably lead to catastrophic disturbance of the system's stability. It is not difficult, however, to find cases where monocultures are grown with relatively little difficulty (e.g. wheat grown in the Canadian prairies), though it is equally easy to find cases where pests and diseases result in crop failure (e.g. *Verticillium* wilt of hops in Hereford and Worcester).

Successful agriculture, with its increasing emphasis on decreased diversity, seems to present a direct challenge to the principle of the inherent

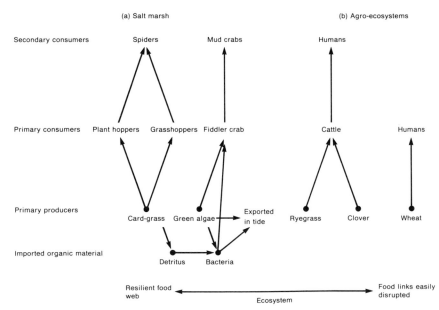

Figure 3.2 Dominant food chains in three ecosystems of decreasing complexity.

instability of monocultures. It appears that agriculture and plantation forestry are much more successful than they ought to be. It is often forgotten that destabilising disturbances from weeds, pests and diseases are often dealt with by pesticide applications. Conditions for maximising plant growth, which usually also maximise plant health, are created by the use of an array of cultural practices and additives (e.g. fertilisers, irrigation and tillage). The idea has been advanced that agricultural ecosystems have been simplified to a point which produces a different form of stability to that which derives from diversity. The stability of the remaining linear food chains, or even the non-existence of feeding relationships, in the crop ecosystem is then readily maintained by carrying out good agricultural practices in greatly simplified monocultures.

If I appear to have provided more theory and questions than facts and answers, I may have been successful in indicating that this aspect of biology needs much more research. One of the most comprehensive examinations of a crop monoculture has been by the Game Conservancy Council on the cereal ecosystems of the Downs in England. The results of their work at the time (1977), indicated that stable yields were accompanied by stable incidences of weeds, of disease and of many arthropod groups (though cereal aphids and mycetophagous (fungus-eating) species were thought to be exceptions). Although the study showed there was no clear evidence of the 'marked instability of agroecosystems', it concluded that the marked upward trend in the use of pesticides may have been an indicator of such instability. Since 1977 there has been a reduction in the amount of pesticides used as the understanding of the ecology of this and other similar systems has increased. It may be that stability (i.e. lack of pests and diseases) can be achieved in the face of ecological theory by skilful and knowledgeable farmers.

3.10   Impact of urbanisation, roads and motorways

The development of urban areas and their road transport networks has had a considerable impact on environmental quality. Urban developments are devastating to the ecosystems in which they are placed, but they leave islands of highly modified ecosystems and create unusual opportunities for plants and animals. What is particularly interesting is the very steep environmental gradients that are established in a tightly packed mosaic of different landscape and habitat types. Urban areas also provide a relatively untapped source of material for examining **island biogeography**. The island biogeography theory, first proposed by R. H. MacArthur and E. O. Wilson in *The theory of island biogeography* (Princetown University Press, 1967), suggests that one of the pivotal problems for living organisms in urban areas is one of dispersal to, and survival in, suitable patches within the mosaic (see figure 3.3). This may explain the deficiency of insect species in city centres, but not the abundance of plants (see later).

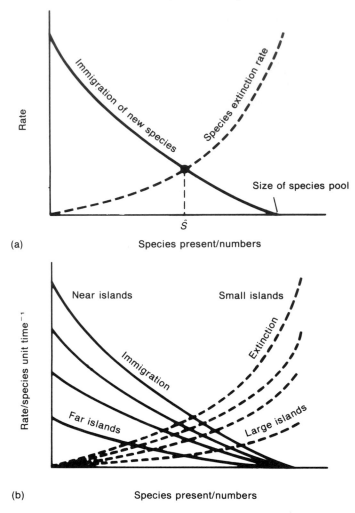

Figure 3.3 Island biogeography theory: (*a*) Equilibrium model for the number of species on a single island (the species equilibrium(s) occurs at the intersection of the curves of immigration of new species and existing species extinction); (b) Equilibrium models where islands of different sizes and different distances from population sources are taken into account – increasing distance from sources reduces the rate of new species arriving, increasing size reduces extinction rates. (Adapted from MacArthur R. H. & Wilson E. O. (1967) *The theory of island biogeography*, Princetown University Press.)

There are a number of unusual features of the flora and fauna of urban areas. A study in Berlin has shown that the expected gradual increase in vegetation cover from the centre to the suburban fringe runs in parallel to a decreasing frequency of alien or introduced plants and an increasing number of rare plants (see table 3.4). It also appears that a higher number of species is found in urbanised areas than in the surrounding countryside, a feature that is also apparent in London, Cambridge (UK) and Hanover (Germany).

Table 3.4. Change in frequency of plant species in response to urban zones in Berlin

			City zone	
	Built-up	Partly built-up	Inner suburbs	Outer suburbs
Vegetation cover (%)	32	55	75	95
Vascular plants (no. km^{-2})	380	424	415	357
Aliens (%)	50	47	43	28
Species introduced before 1500	15	14	14	10
Species introduced after 1500	24	23	21	16
Rare species (no. km^{-2})	17	23	35	58

Source: Sukopp H. *et al.* 1979. The soil, flora and vegetation of Berlin's wastelands. In Laurie I. C. (ed.) *Nature in cities,* John Wiley.

Many successful urban plants, for example rose bay willow herb (*Chamerion angustifolium*), coltsfoot (*Tussilago farfara*), michaelmas daisy (*Aster × salignus*), toadflaxes (*Chaenorhinum* spp. and *Cymbalaria* spp.), golden rod (*Solidago canadensis*), wormwood (*Artemisia absinthum*), common ragwort (*Senecio jacobeae*), Oxford ragwort (*S. squalidus*) and thistles (*Carduus* spp. and *Cirsium* spp.), are the weeds of the gardener. They are well adapted to frequent disturbance, poor quality soils and other stressful environmental factors, and have considerable powers of long-distance dispersal with small, wind-blown seeds. These plants are classified by plant ecologists as **ruderals**. Other successful city dwellers have originated from garden escapes. On the other hand, some assemblages of plants are poorly represented in urban areas. These are often those of later successional stages; plants of the woodland ground zone; hedgerow and woodland edge species; understorey shrubs; and species associated with meadows and rough grassland.

A different response is shown by insects. More species of ground-dwelling arthropods are found in gardens in the suburbs than in the city centre (see figure 3.4). The alien plants more frequent in the city centre have been introduced without their normal insect fauna, and native insects may not be well adapted for living on them. One significant factor not favourable to ground insects is the absence of a well-developed litter layer in inner-city areas.

The bird community of urban areas is different to that of the surounding countryside. It has been argued that larger birds need larger territories. As the size of 'green' patches in most urban areas declines towards the centre, the bird communities that are found in city centres will, therefore, be deficient in large-sized birds. This was found to be the case in London.

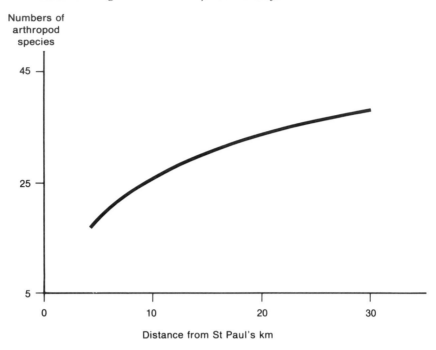

Figure 3.4 Relationship between number of species of ground-dwelling arthropods and distance from London city centre. (Adapted from Davies B. N. K. (1979) in *London Naturalist* **58**:15–24.)

There are a number of ubiquitous town-dweller birds, for example starling (*Sturnus vulgaris*), feral pigeon (*Columbia livia*) and, pre-eminently, house sparrow (*Passer domesticus*). The last two generalist species are pre-adapted for living close to humans. Starlings use high buildings and the city heat island effect to provide roosting sites. A number of birds have developed specialised techniques for exploiting food resources in urban areas, for example tits (*Parus* spp.) opening milk bottles and magpies (*Pica pica*) milk cartons. Omnivorous gulls (Laridae) scavenge rubbish tips and other generalist species, such as jackdaw (*Corvus monedula*), carrion crow (*C. corone*), rook (*C. frugilepus*), and jay (*Garrulus glandarius*) are faring increasingly well in urban areas, free from the persecution that is more frequent in the countryside. A number of birds, for example kittiwake (*Rissa tridactyla*), kestrel (*Falco tinnunculus*), peregrine falcon (*F. peregrinus*) and black redstart (*Phoenicurus ochruros*), use tall buildings as substitutes for cliff nesting sites.

The classic example of **evolutionary change** in response to urbanisation has been the work by H. B. Kettlewell in the 1950s on the peppered moth (*Biston betularia*). This species rests during the day on the trunks of trees. In clean air conditions, tree trunks are covered in lichens and are pale in colour, but as a result of industrial pollution trunks loose their lichen cover and are blackened by grime. A dark (or melanic) morph of the moth, var. *carbonaria*, normally rare in rural environments, became dominant in urban areas in Manchester as a result of differential predation by birds. The dark morph is effectively camouflaged on blackened, lichen-free trunks, whereas the light morph is readily detected by birds in cities. Since the mid-1970s there has been a reversal in the frequency of the melanic form in Manchester that is thought to be related to the spread of a lichen, *Lecanora conizaeoides*, which offers neither morph any camouflage protection. Several other arthropods have melanic forms in urban areas. This type of evolutionary response has also been seen in plants. Research has shown that lead-tolerant strains of bent grass (*Agrostis capillaris*) have appeared in soil by 'spaghetti junction', the convergence of the M5 and M6 motorways in Birmingham, UK, as a result of the selection pressure of toxic lead from anti-knock compounds in petrol.

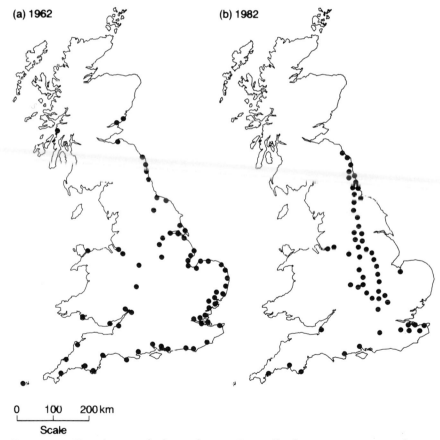

(a) 1962

(b) 1982

0   100   200 km

Scale

Figure 3.5 Distribution of salt marsh grass (*Puccinellia distans*) (*a*) as in 1962; (*b*) on roadsides in 1982. Compare the distribution in (*b*) with a map showing the M1, A1, M2, M20 and A2 trunk roads. (Redrawn from Perring F. H. & Walters S. M. (1962) *Atlas of the British flora*, Nelson; and Scott N. E. & Davison A. W. (1982) in *Watsonia* **14**:41–52.)

Rock salt is used extensively for de-icing roads and the effects of the build-up of sodium chloride (NaCl) in soils next to roads is of considerable interest to ecologists. The golden yellow strip of dandelions (*Taraxacum officinale* agg.) along some road edges probably results from the presence of salt-tolerant strains of dandelion growing where salt and/or herbicides have reduced competition from grasses. Some roadside soils have such high concentrations of salt that salt marsh plants have spread along road networks into the centre of the UK (see figure 3.5). A wide range of maritime species has been recorded from road verges (see table 3.5).

The development of major road systems in the UK has produced significant opportunities for wildlife and creative conservation (see chapter 5), and opened up corridors for species to travel along in parallel with road traffic. Verges are planted with or develop interesting plant communities which provide habitats for a wide range of plants and animals, for example the kestrel (*Falco tinnunculus*), which feeds on small mammals living in the rough grassland areas.

Table 3.5. Plants from maritime habitats occurring on roadsides in Britain

Scientific name	Common name
Armeria maritima	Thrift
Aster tripolium	Sea aster
Atriplex littoralis	Grass leaved orache
Atriplex portaculacoides	Sea purslane
Bupleurum tenuissimum	Slender hare's-ear
Catapodium marinum	Sea fern-grass
Cochlearia danica	Danish scurvygrass
Cochlearia officinalis	Common scurvygrass
Elymus antherica	Sea couch
Hordeum marinum	Sea barley
Juncus gerardii	Saltmarsh rush
Parapholis strigosa	Hard grass
Plantago coronopus	Buck's horn plantain
Plantago maritima	Sea plantain
Puccinellia distans	Reflexed saltmarsh-grass
Puccinellia fasciculata	Borrer's saltmarsh-grass
Puccinellia maritima	Common saltmarsh-grass
Puccinellia rupestris	Stiff saltmarsh-grass
Spergularia marina	Lesser sea-spurrey
Spergularia media	Greater sea-spurrey
Suaeda maritima	Annual sea-blight
Agaricus bernardii	Toadstool

Source: Scott N. E. & Davison A. W. 1982. De-icing salt and the invasion of road verges by maritime plants, *Watsonia* **15**:41–52; Scott N. E. 1985. The updated distribution of maritime species on British roadsides, *Watsonia* **14**:381–386.

Consequences of desertification, deforestation and afforestation

4.1 Phenomenon of desertification

Deserts are dry areas with few plants and can be conveniently separated from other vegetation types on the basis of rainfall and temperature. They are found where mean annual rainfall is below about 50 mm and mean annual temperature is above 15 °C. The term **desertification** was used initially (1949) in reference to the increasing extension of deserts into semi-arid lands. In the 1980s and 1990s, authorities have begun to question the extent or even existence of the desertification problem. The term desertification may imply a 'once and for all' process on a massive scale, but what seems to happen on the ground (in areas where desertification appears to be occurring) is the development of areas of land degradation, in some cases quite severe, but which with care and two or three good rainy seasons might return to their former status.

Here is the suggestion, discussed by J. A. Binns in 'Is desertification a myth?' (*Geography* **75** : 106–13 (1990)), that the phenomenon is linked with lack of rainfall (i.e. drought) and land utilisation of a kind that damages the environment. Perhaps the critical point, which is rarely stressed, is that the degradation (desertification) occurs in areas where rainfall is usually sufficient to support at least a sparse vegetation cover.

The 'approximate desert boundaries' in the Sudan (see figure 4.1) suggest the desert in Sudan moved south by about 120 km between 1958 and 1975. A feature not often noted is the presence of old sand dunes further south than the 1975 boundary, suggesting that the desert may have extended further south in the past. The aerial survey, from which the 1975 boundary was deduced, was carried out in drought conditions. Later studies have shown that little long-term damage was done to the vegetation by the drought. J. A. Binns concluded that desertification 'is much less widespread than has often been portrayed in the media and areas have frequently been classified as desertified on the basis of incomplete evidence and statistics. In many cases . . . the term "desertification" has been used when "land degradation" would have been more appropriate.'

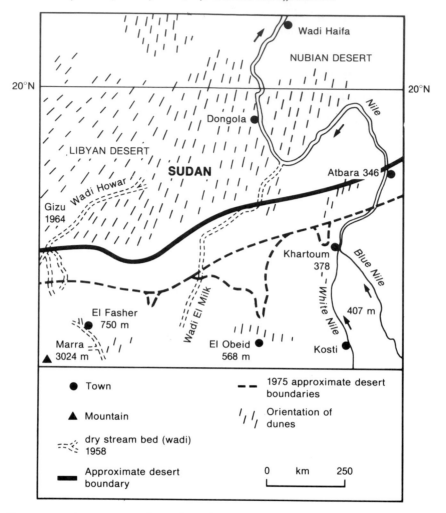

Figure 4.1 Approximate desert boundaries in 1958 and 1975 in the northern Sudan. Note the presence of dune ridges south of the 1975 boundary. (Redrawn from Rapp A. *et al.* (1976) in *Ecological Bulletin* **24**.)

4.2   Ecology of desertification

Nevertheless degradation, often exacerbated by drought conditions, does occur in semi-arid regions, producing large areas more or less devoid of plant life, with soils exposed to wind erosion. The terrible plight of the peoples of the horn of Africa have been graphically displayed in our own living rooms on television. It is difficult to believe that the soil of Ethiopia could be restored to agricultural productivity even in the absence of drought, but there is little evidence to suggest that this is not possible. In 1984, U. Hellden, a Swedish research worker, reported that the drought of 1962–79 in

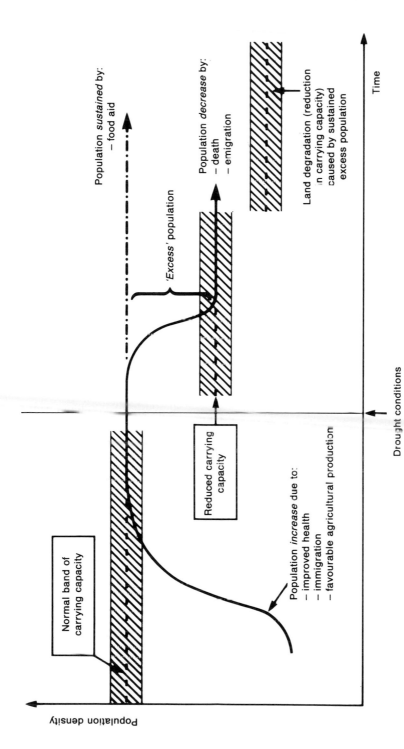

Figure 4.2 Population responses to drought conditions in semi-arid, desert margin zones in relation to environmental carrying capacity.

Sudan had created no long-lasting desert conditions; that no woody plant species had disappeared from the area; and that ecological zones had not shifted. He concluded that the impact of the drought was short-lasting and was followed by a fast land production recovery.

It is not difficult to produce a list of features that lead to land degradation in semi-arid zones. The question can be approached ecologically by considering the land's carrying capacity – the maximum population density that agricultural production can sustain (see figure 4.2). The carrying capacity of the environment in desert and semi-desert regions is subject to two main threats, the first unpredictable, the second probably uncontrollable:

1 The impact of unusual climatic or weather conditions (most often drought, but occasionally floods).
2 Increased human population growth, which places increasing demands on food production and fuel requirements. Food production often depends on animals and may lead to overgrazing. Human population growth can result from a response to good food production, immigration, or increased survival rates due to improved health care or food imports.

An example of the interaction of a variety of factors and the way in which these can affect populations in semi-arid regions has been described for the Kordofan and Darfur areas of northern Sudan. The people of this area were essentially nomadic, moving to the wetter south in September as the grasslands of the north withered in the dry season, returning for the July–August rainy season. However, governments have attempted to sedentarise the nomads. Provision of additional water resources to support changing land-use resulted in a growing population and an increase in the numbers of livestock. Settled agriculture and arable farming have restricted access of the remaining nomads to their traditional lands. A sequence of environmental disasters, presented in a simplified form below, were a consequence:

1 There was widespread overgrazing.
2 Within 2 km of water holes very little vegetation was left at all and within 5 km the impact of overgrazing was intense.
3 There was an increasing demand for fuel, which resulted in the indiscriminate cutting of all woody plants, the suppression of regrowth and a further reduction in vegetation cover. Acacia (*Acacia* spp.) trees, which produced gum arabic, an important export crop for the area, decreased in number through browsing and cutting, and family incomes fell.
4 The loss of ground vegetation and tree cover allowed wind erosion to remove soil, which then blew over cultivated areas, interrupted the normal annual growth of grasses and inhibited replanting efforts.

This situation had developed in a 25-year period up to 1970, but little was done about it until the disastrous droughts of the early 1970s reduced food production to nothing. The consequences were mass migration, famine and death, although this was mercifully mitigated by food aid from overseas countries.

4.3   Solution of desertification problems

In parallel to the argument over the subject of desertification itself, there is a variety of views over what can be done to prevent it or halt its spread. Desertification and land degradation problems are a product of a series of complex interactions between the subsistence agriculture and social structures of the people that inhabit semi-arid zones and the intractable dilemma of unpredictable drought. In 1935 E. P. Stebbing proposed in 'The encroaching Sahara' (*Geographical Journal* **85**:506–24) that desert spread in Africa could be combated by planting forest belts around the edge of the Sahara Desert. This view fell into disfavour, largely because of the size of the task and the inability to achieve political consensus in a divided continent. Many authorities believed that careful attention to land-use throughout the semi-arid zone would solve the problem. In 1990 it was suggested there was an urgent need to examine links between management systems and land productivity, implying that attention to the relationships of people and land was of critical importance. This must surely, be the case. There has been, however, a recent increase in interest in modifications of E. P. Stebbing's idea and several successful tree-planting schemes for the rehabilitation of degraded semi-arid and savannah land have been initiated. The Kenyan Green Belt Movement, started in 1974, has shown the benefits that can ensue from planting trees in semi-arid zones. This project has been driven along by Professor Wangari Maathai. She was aided by the women of Kenya, the traditional wood-gatherers, who appreciated the significance of the problem at first hand. Tree nurseries, 600 in number, were established, 7 million trees have been planted and some 50 000 people are involved.

Some of the advantages of tree planting are:

- reduction of soil losses caused by wind erosion
- improvement of fuel-wood supplies, a significant problem in Africa
- provision of stock food from foliage on cut branches
- stabilisation of sand dunes
- improvement of soil properties
- improvement in productivity of adjacent arable crops

It is often hoped that the presence of trees will have such a significant impact that rainfall, run-off patterns and soil moisture content will change and thus decrease local aridity. However, trees will only grow in areas with adequate levels of rainfall and tree planting can only be successful in the more favourable semi-arid areas.

An ecologist could suggest only two solutions to the land degradation process in semi-arid regions:

1 To take steps to maintain the population density of humans and their grazing herds to a level *below* the long-term carrying capacity of the environment.

2 To increase the carrying capacity of the land by increasing agricultural productivity.

A technologist might also refine this argument by suggesting that short-term deficits in food production could be overcome by importing food from less climate-susceptible areas or by the provision of storage facilities for carrying over surplus production from 'good' years to 'bad'. Humans have few options: population density is the consequence of births and immigration on the one hand, and death and emigration on the other. It appears that, if deaths from starvation which result from the vagaries of food production in semi-arid regions are to be avoided, the only answer is to use patterns of social behaviour or our understanding of medicine to reduce the number of recruits to the population. It is essential to maintain the population balance below the carrying capacity of the environment in which these populations live. It is rather more easy to write this than to actually do it; there are enormous religious, social and educational difficulties to overcome before this could be achieved. One extremely significant factor is that children are seen as an important resource because of their contribution to the productivity of family units. The question of a population balance is a nettle that has to be grasped, not by ecologists, not by the United Nations, not by financially prosperous countries, but by the people and politicians of the arid zones themselves.

On a more optimistic note, it is not difficult to find examples of situations where the carrying capacity of deserts has been increased. The production of large quantities of food from the irrigation of the Negev Desert by the Israelis, sufficient not only for local consumption but also for export, is one of the more notable examples. Such schemes do depend on many factors including: the presence of an adequate water supply; political will and planning on a very large scale; high technical and engineering skills; a detailed knowledge of local hydrology and soil structure; and the water and nutrient requirements of plants. The major problems facing such schemes in arid zones are the depletion and pollution of underground water resources; the movement of sea water into underground water supplies; and the creation of saline soils by surface evaporation. With detailed knowledge and careful planning these pitfalls can be avoided and the desert made 'to bloom'.

4.4   Scale of deforestation

Forests have been cleared for millennia; large areas of the globe that have a climatic regime and soils that would permit the development of a forest vegetation type are now used for pasture, arable farming or orchards. In Britain, which would naturally be almost entirely wooded, only about 10% is forested. Between 1958 and 1980, it has been estimated there was a *net loss of carbon* from forests to the atmosphere as a result of the continuation of changes to the world's forest cover and a continuing decline in biomass of forest vegetation types and their replacement with some other kind of land-use or vegetation type (see table 4.1). A net loss to the atmosphere of 57.3×10^9 million tonnes carbon for the 22-year period is mainly a result of clearing forests for cultivation or grazing. The carbon store in arable crops or grassland vegetation is much lower than that found in forests, by a factor of between 20 and 100 times.

The biggest losses, in the 1990s, occur as a result of deforestation in Latin America and tropical Africa. North American forest companies have realised that they cannot continue to 'mine' their forests at the same rate as even 20 years ago and are now (1990s) investing in the regeneration of cut-over forests and in plantation forestry. The current rate of forest loss on a global scale is probably as large as it has ever been. It has been estimated that net global deforestation between the pre-industrial period (about 1750) and 1954 was 33%, but in the late 1980s it was about 1% per year. Estimates put the annual decline in the 1990s in tropical rainforest areas to be somewhere between 0.5% and 3%. The grim march of global deforestation is echoed in facts like these:

Table 4.1. Transfers of carbon to the atmosphere as a result of forest activities for the period 1958–80

Forest activities	Carbon (10⁹ million tonnes)
Forest clearing and cultivation	− 29.1
Decay of wood from forests	− 11.1
Forest clearing and grazing	− 5.9
Harvest of forests	− 58.3
Regrowth of harvested forest	+ 45.8
Net abandonment and afforestation	+ 1.3
Total transfer	− 57.5
(Burning of fossil fuels	− 85.5)

−   Loss to the atmosphere.
+   Fixation from the atmosphere.
Source: Freedman B. (1989, modified from Houghton R. A. *et al.* 1983. Changes in the carbon content of terrestrial biota and soils between 1860 and 1980. *Ecological Monographs* **53**:235–62.

Every year, 5 million hectares of Asian forest are lost and millions more degraded by improper use. The total area of forest in Thailand was reduced from 58.3% of the country in 1952 to 39% by 1973 and 33% by 1978. Afghanistan is being deforested so rapidly that the country could become essentially barren by 1990–1995. For all practical purposes, Malaysia's forests could be gone by 1990. Nepal is likely to be denuded by the end of the century.

Kimmins J. P. 1987 *Forest Ecology*, Collier Macmillan.

Kimmins' text is a model of careful and substantiated explanation of facts on forest ecology and not an emotive catalogue of disasters; the message behind these facts is real and must be acknowledged.

4.5   Problems caused by deforestation and their solution

There are a number of both long- and short-term consequences of deforestation (see Freedman (1989)).

1   Long-term

- potential decline in fertility of the site due to nutrient losses
- alteration of wildlife habitat
- potential loss of old-growth forest habitat
- climatic change and disruption of the global carbon cycle

2   Short-term

- increase in erosion
- changes in watershed hydrology
- inadequate regeneration of forests
- temporary changes in wildlife habitat

Forests are normally very conservative ecosystems. Much of the nutrient capital is sequestered (made unavailable) in dead plant material. Nutrients released by decomposition processes are taken up by plants as quickly as they are mineralised and are then used for growth. The mat of plant roots binds soil together and the leaf cover reduces the impact of raindrops on the soil surface, both features reducing soil erosion. The organic matter in the soil increases its water-holding capacity and much of rainfall intercepted by the canopy percolates down to the ground slowly or is evaporated back into the atmosphere, thus reducing the severity and rapidity of run-off from the catchment. Well-developed woodland or forest ecosystems are, therefore, excellent at preventing loss of nutrient capital, reducing soil erosion and preventing land degradation. The consequences of deforestation can often be a major environmental concern.

One of the most careful studies of the influence of deforestation on the environment was carried out on the Hubbard Brook, New Hampshire, USA.

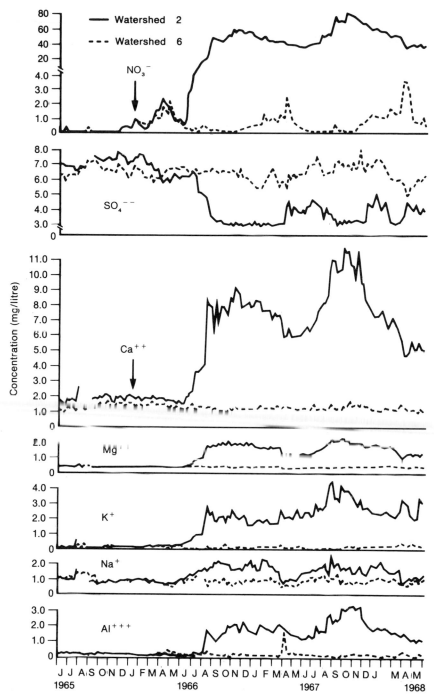

Figure 4.3 Concentration of ions in outflow from catchment 2 (treated) and catchment 6 (control) from the Hubbard Brook, New Hampshire. Note the change in the scale of the axis for the nitrate ion. (From Likens G. E. *et al.* (1970) in *Ecological Monographs* **40**:23–47.)

The Hubbard Brook catchment area was divided into a number of small watersheds, each of which received a different experimental treatment. Amongst these treatments, one watershed (15.6 ha) had its vegetation cut down but left in place in winter and was treated with a herbicide in the three following summers to prevent any regrowth. A second area of similar size was left untreated as an experimental control. The biogeochemistry of the watersheds were carefully monitored. The consequences of these dramatic treatments on the chemistry of the water leaving the watershed is shown in figure 4.3. The normal small nutrient losses in drainage from forested watersheds were replaced by mass leakage of some, but not all, plant nutrients following destruction of the vegetation cover (see table 4.2).

Apart from the changes in water chemistry, the total water flow from the treated (deforested) watershed increased by about 31% over the three years after cutting. This represents the water that would have been returned to the atmosphere by evapotranspiration. There was also an increase in losses of particulate matter, despite the fact that the experiment was carried out so that erosion was minimised.

The Hubbard Brook data have been used uncritically in the past to show the likely consequences of harvesting forests by clearfelling. The authors of the work were so concerned at this mis-use of their data that they

Table 4.2. Net losses of nutrients (streamwater outputs minus atmospheric inputs) for two watersheds of Hubbard Brook, from summer 1966 to summer 1969

	Net losses (kg ha^{-1})	
Element	*Deforested watershed*	*Control watershed*
Ca^{2+}	77.7	9.0
Mg^{2+}	15.6	2.6
K^+	30.3	1.5
Na^+	15.4	6.1
Al^{3+}	21.1	3.0
NH_4^+-N[a]	-1.6	-2.2
NO_3^--N[b]	114.1	-2.3
$SO_4^{2-}-S$[c]	2.8	4.1
Cl^-	1.7	-1.2

—   Indicates net gain rather than loss.
[a] NH_4^+-N Loss of nitrogen as ammonium ion.
[b] NO_3^--N Loss of nitrogen as nitrate ion.
[c] $SO_4^{2-}-S$ Loss of sulphur as sulphate ion.
Source: Bormann F. H. & Likens G. E. 1979. *Pattern and process in a forested ecosystem*, Springer-Verlag.

wrote a paper explaining that the consequences of their experimental treatments were not the same as would be produced by forest harvesting and that it was incorrect to extrapolate from their results to normal forestry practices. Studies similar to those at Hubbard Brook have been carried out on normally harvested watersheds. Some have shown comparable or, more frequently, much lower losses of nutrients following harvest; a few have shown insignificant nutrient losses. It appears that nutrient losses are least when small proportions of watersheds are harvested, when the productivity of regrowth is high, and if disturbance caused by felling and extraction is minimised. The type of forest, its constituent species, hydrological conditions and climate also influence nutrient losses. A good understanding of catchment conditions and careful harvesting can reduce environmental damage to insignificant levels, particularly if steps are taken to re-create high canopy forest as quickly as possible. The telescoping of successional processes into as short a time as possible has the duel benefit of decreasing harvest intervals and minimising environmental damage through nutrient loss. This can be done by planting the next crop directly after clearfelling.

4.6 Special significance of tropical rainforests

The loss of tropical rainforest merits special attention for a number of reasons:

1 Rainforests contain about 50% of the Earth's standing timber.
2 It was estimated that they have the potential to produce 75% of the world's wood products.
3 They contain a large gene pool of plant resources. Many species have not even been described; their potential for the production of food, fibre, and pharmaceutical or industrial biochemicals is unknown.
4 They produce a wide variety of useful forest produce, for example timber, brazil nuts, drugs and fruits.
5 They are a huge store for carbon and a sink for atmospheric carbon dioxide.
6 On a global scale tropical rainforests play an important part in biogeochemical cycling, notably in the hydrological cycle and in carbon cycling. Of the carbon dioxide currently entering the atmosphere, 30% is from deforestation, mainly from tropical rainforest. It has been estimated that destruction of the remaining rainforest will increase atmospheric concentrations of carbon dioxide (a greenhouse gas) by 50%.
7 Rainforests are important in conserving soil nutrients and preventing large-scale erosion in regions with high rainfall and with soils which are often readily leached.

It has been estimated that at present rates, apart from areas put aside for reserves, tropical rainforests may have all but disappeared some time between the end of the twentieth and the middle of the twenty-first centuries. The environmental difficulties associated with deforestation (see above) generally appear to be compounded in tropical rainforest regions.

4.7   Traditional utilisation of tropical rainforest

Traditional forest utilisation was either based on hunter–gatherer cultures, on small-scale slash-and-burn agriculture, or a combination of both. Hunter–gatherers would have had a minimal impact on the forest environment. In the slash-and-burn system small patches of cleared forests were used for growing crops, but productivity fell dramatically after the first harvest due to nutrient removal in crops and by rain (leaching), the breakdown of soil structure, erosion, increasing attacks of insect and fungal pests, and growing competition from invading weeds. After food production declined, the people moved on to another small patch and the original clearing slowly reverted to forest again. This system of utilisation caused few environmental problems and was capable of supporting low-density populations, about $5 \, km^{-2}$. In general the soils of the tropical rainforest appear to be unable to sustain cultivation indefinitely and many large-scale agricultural initiatives in them have failed. Failure then drives the cultivators to fell and burn more forest and further degradation follows. The tragedy of the tropical rainforests is that attempts at utilising the land on which the forests stand have produced failure on a large scale and the governments that have induced their citizens to be involved in failure are trapped by the size of the problem and their own poverty.

4.8   Tropical rainforests exploited

Some spectacular examples of disastrous exploitation of tropical rainforests are found in Brazil and neighbouring countries of the Amazon basin. Attempts have been made to exploit the forests on a large scale for a number of purposes, for example:

1 development of rubber plantations;
2 timber extraction;
3 conversion to agriculture for cash crops (coffee, cocoa, pepper and oil palm) particularly along river courses, for cattle ranching and for peasant farming (the most dramatic influences have been on the Brazilian Atlantic Coast forests, which have more or less gone, and in the Rondônia and Acre regions of the Amazonian basin);

4 extraction of minerals, most notably bauxite for the production of aluminium around Jaru and iron ore at Carajás; and

5 pulp and paper manufacture, associated with the aluminium extraction at Jaru.

In the Amazon any significant disruption of the forests almost always results in the disruption of a closed ecological cycle, leakage of nutrients, and severe land degradation. Unfortunately, most attempts to exploit the Amazon rainforest, whether instigated by the Brazilian government, large multi-national companies, business entrepreneurs, cattle ranchers or migrating peasant farmers, have ended in environmental degradation. The consequences of deforestation are soil infertility, floods, soil erosion, high sediment loads in rivers and silting of river beds and hydro-electric dams.

The scale of the problem is very large, measured either in the numbers of people involved or the area of forest damaged. The developers of the Jaru bauxite/timber extraction/wood pulp/agriculture initiative purchased 4 million hectares of forest. The scheme involved the development of 4 500 km of roads, four towns, an airport, a railway, port facilities, schools and hospitals, and produced almost 10 million settlers by 1982. The scheme was not successful. Many of the settlers were left to survive by migrating further into the forest to clear more land for a short-lived agricultural return – compounding problems still further. Access to the centre of the forest is now possible as a result of the construction of the Trans-Amazonia Highway from the Atlantic Ocean to the Pacific. This has drawn peasant farmers into the previously inaccessible depths of the forest in Rondânia and Arre to follow the inevitable cycle of forest destruction, temporary cultivations, soil erosion and further migration.

Tropical rainforest destruction is not confined to Amazonia, although in some areas its consequences may not be as severe, as some rainforest soils appear capable of sustaining cultivation. The fact that most rainforests will be gone in a matter of decades is known and recognised by the authorities, but there has been no change in the rate of destruction and there are predictions that the rate of deforestation will increase.

Nevertheless, there are glimmers of hope. The Brazilian government plans to retain 1.8 million km² of its tropical rainforest covered by natural vegetation and had established 87 644 km² of natural parks, biological reserves and ecological stations by 1982. Concern was expressed by Brazilian ecologists that a rapidly growing population, problems of enforcing the law and protecting the forests, and a lack of scientific knowledge, posed considerable difficulties for conservation of the remaining rainforest. In other parts of the world it is possible to be more optimistic; reserves that are being set aside have better protection and steps are even being taken to regenerate tropical forests (although the most successful project to date (1991) has been with tropical *dry* forest, in Costa Rica).

Three scenarios (see table 4.3) predict the transfers of carbon dioxide to

Table 4.3. Net annual transfer of carbon to the atmosphere (billion million tonnes (bmT) per year) under different strategies of tropical forest management

| | *Strategies* | | |
	1	*2*	*3*
		Stop removal of rainforest	
Source of carbon to the atmosphere	*Current land use practices*	*Reforestation to accumulate carbon on land*	*Fossil fuels replaced with wood fuels*
Fossil fuel	5.6	5.6	0
Deforestation	1.5–3.0	0	0
Reforestation	0	− 1.5	0
Plantations	0	0	0*
Total release of carbon to atmosphere	7.0–9.0	4.0	0

* This represents a balance between 6.9 bmT of carbon released annually from the burning of 15×10^9 tonnes of wood harvested each year from 50 million hectares of plantation, and 6.9 bmT carbon accumulated annually in 500–1000 million hectares of plantation regrowth.
Source: Houghton R. A. Role of forests affecting greenhouse gas composition. In Wyman R. L. (ed.) (1991).

the atmosphere under different tropical rainforest management strategies. Only the third strategy, replacing the energy demands met by fossil fuel use with energy derived from plantation forestry, provides a permanent solution to stabilisation of carbon dioxide levels in the atmosphere. Who is going to choose, and implement, any one of these scenarios? Is inertia going to choose the first scenario?

4.9   Why plant conifers in the uplands of UK?

Having understood that deforestation can have serious consequences for the environment, we may be surprised to find that afforestation in the UK has also caused concern. The UK produces only 12–13% of its own requirement of wood and wood products and has to spend £7 billion (1991 figure) on imports to make up the deficiency. Three-quarters of the woods used are softwoods (coniferous species) and half the wood or wood products imported are for paper or paper products. Given these facts and the knowledge that only 10% of the country is forested compared with an average figure for Europe of 25%, it is understandable that there has been a long-standing pressure, encouraged at government level, for the nation to plant more trees. The problems of afforestation in the UK have to be seen in the light of an understandable requirement to increase the volume of forest produce.

It has been a long-standing and world-wide phenomenon that land acquired and used for forestry has been that which appears to be of limited use for anything else − land of low inherent fertility and/or with contours that make other land uses difficult. This has meant in the UK that most forest planting has been carried out in upland areas. Moreover, the relatively short rotation times of softwoods in comparison with hardwoods, the pulp and timber industry being equipped to process softwoods, and the versatility of softwood produce, ensure that forest developments will use coniferous plantations rather than deciduous broad-leaved woodlands. The species most frequently planted are Sitka spruce (*Picea sitchensis*), lodgepole pine (*Pinus contorta*), Norway spruce, (*Picea abies*), Scots pine (*Pinus sylvestris*) and larches (*Larix* spp.) (in the uplands almost entirely the first two species).

4.10 Upland afforestation and environmental concerns

The environmental concerns about **upland afforestation** arise from two perspectives:

1 the changes in landscape that result from large-scale afforestation;
2 the consequences of afforestation on wildlife values and nature conservation − this concern has been focused on populations and communities of birds and, more recently, on the loss of upland peat bog plant communities.

The uplands consist of rough grassland, heather moorland and blanket peat bog and are the product of forest clearance. They are referred to as **degraded vegetation types** and are maintained as plagioclimaxes by burning and grazing. If neglected, the vegetation would slowly return to the climax forest of oak (*Quercus* spp.) or Scots pine (*Pinus sylvestris*). Afforestation markedly reduces the successional time scale and, of course, establishes a quite different type of forest. At their worst, conifer plantations present a landscape of square blocks of uniformly coloured foliage, with very little species richness and very low conservation interest. These effects can be minimised by sympathetic, well-planned planting and appropriate management and harvesting techniques.

Afforestation of uplands with conifers has been shown to:

1 increase the acidity of water drainage from forested catchments, with a consequent increase in concentrations of aluminium and a decline in levels of available nitrogen, phosphorus and calcium in the soil. This

Table 4.4. Seventy-one bird species associated with the British uplands and potential vulnerability to afforestation

Breed mainly in montane or sub-montane habitat	Opportunistic species with major niches in mountains and moorland	Use upland lakes, rivers and streams	Have at least a foothold in the uplands*
Ptarmigan (Lagopus mutus)	Peregrine falcon (Falco peregrinus)[1]	Black-throated diver (Gavia arctica)[1,3]	Jackdaw (Corvus monedula)
Dotterel (Charadrius morinellus)	Raven (Corvus corax)[1,2]	Red-throated diver (Gavia stellata)[1,3]	Tree pipit (Anthus trivialis)
Snow bunting (Plectrophenax nivalis)	Buzzard (Buteo buteo)[1,2]	Wigeon (Anas penelope)[1]	Grasshopper warbler (Locustella naevia)
Red grouse (Lagopus lagopus scoticus)[1,2]	Kestrel (Falco tinnunculus)	Goosander (Mergus merganser)	Pied wagtail (Motacilla alba)
Golden plover (Pluvialis apricaria)[1,2]	Red kite (Milvus milvus)[1]	Red-breasted merganser (Mergus serrator)[1]	Mistle thrush (Turdus viscivorus)
Dunlin (Calidris alpina)[1,2]	Carrion/Hooded crows (Corvus corone)	Common scoter (Melanitta nigra)[1]	Song thrush (Turdus philomelos)
Twite (Acanthis flavirostris)[1,3]	Meadow pipit (Anthus pratensis)	Teal (Anas crecca)	Oystercatcher (Haematopus ostralegus)
Whimbrel (Numenius phaeopus)	Skylark (Alauda arvensis)[1,2]	Dipper (Cinclus cinclus)[1,3]	Ringed plover (Charadrius hiaticula)
Red-necked phalarope (Phalaropus lobatus)	Wren (Troglodytes troglodytes)	Grey wagtail (Motacilla cinerea)	Herring gull (Larus argentatus)
Arctic skua (Stercorarius parasiticus)[1,3]	Wheatear (Oenanthe oenanthe)[1,2]	Greylag goose (Anser anser)[1]	Lesser black-backed gull (Larus fuscus)
Great skua (Stercorarius skua)[1]	Whinchat (Saxicola rubetra)[1]	Common sandpiper (Actitis hypoleucos)	Great black-backed gull (Larus marinus)
Greenshank (Tringa nebularia)[1,2]	Stonechat (Saxicola torquata)[1,3]	Common gull (Larus canus)	Stock dove (Columba oenas)
Wood sandpiper (Tringa glareola)	Cuckoo (Cuculus canorus)	Mallard (Anas platyrhynchos)	Nightjar (Caprimulgus europaeus)
Temminck's stint (Calidris temminckii)	Lapwing (Vanellus vanellus)[1,2]	Black-headed gull (Larus ridibundus)	Whitethroat (Sylvia communis)
Ring ouzel (Turdus torquatus)[1,2]	Snipe (Gallinago gallinago)[1,2]	Slavonian grebe (Podiceps auritus)	Tawny owl (Strix aluco)
Golden eagle (Aquila chrysaetos)[1,3]	Redshank (Tringa totanus)[1,2]		Willow warbler (Phylloscopus trochilus)
Merlin (Falco columbarius)[1,2]	Curlew (Numenius arquata)[1,2]		Redwing (Turdus iliacus)
Hen harrier (Circus cyaneus)[1]	Black grouse (Tetrao tetrix)		Fieldfare (Turdus pilaris)
Short-eared owl (Asio flammeus)[1]	Chough (Pyrrhocorax pyrrhocorax)[1,3]		

* List of species somewhat subjective. At least another 22 species associated with woodland or scrub could be added (if upland woods were more widespread and at higher altitudes within the sub-montane zone some of their birds would have significant footholds in the uplands). Rare species (e.g. snowy owl (Nyctea scandiaca) and purple sandpiper (Calidris maritima)) have been excluded.

1 The 32 species potentially at some risk from afforestation.

2 The 14 species eradicated or substantially reduced in distribution by afforestation.

3 The 8 species likely to decline through further expansion (this is a minimum estimate).

Source: Thompson D.B.A. et al. 1988. Afforestation and upland birds. In Usher M.B. & Thompson D.B.A. Ecological change in the uplands, Blackwell Scientific Publications.

problem is of greater significance where soils are poor and have a low buffering capacity and where acid rainfall is prevalent.

2 reduce the yield of water in catchments due to losses, as high as 25–30%, resulting from increased evapotranspiration. This can be a difficulty if the forests are developed in the catchments of reservoirs or rivers used for water supply. Conversely this may be an advantage in reducing flood frequency.

3 alter the hydrology of the catchment areas in other ways, for example as a consequence of the drainage often necessary for successful tree establishment in upland areas.

4 increase the levels of residues in water of herbicides (used for weed control when the trees are being planted), pesticides (used to control forest pests, e.g. caterpillars of the pine beauty moth (*Panolis flammea*) and forest fertilisers (most frequently urea, ammonium nitrate and phosphate in upland areas).

Concern about changes in upland bird communities as a result of afforestation has generated considerable debate. Birds of rough grassland, heather moorland and bog country will be replaced by species adapted to living in forests (see table 4.4 for a résumé of birds considered vulnerable to upland afforestation), but there are some other, less obvious, significant influences. These have been described in a useful model by research workers from the Nature Conservancy Council (see figure 4.4). The species that are threatened by afforestation are often of high conservation interest. The more dramatic of these (e.g. golden eagle (*Aquila chrysaetos*) red grouse (*Lagopus lagopus*), red kite (*Milvus milvus*) and raven (*Corvus corax*)) are often relatively rare and/or large birds with requirements for extended areas of suitable habitat. Most of the species that will be found in maturing conifer plantations are likely to be common species of less conservation interest (e.g. coal tit (*Parus ater*), willow warbler (*Phylloscopus trochilus*) and chaffinch (*Fringilla coelebs*)), although some less-common birds may also become more abundant (e.g. sparrow hawk (*Accipiter nisus*), goldcrest (*Regulus regulus*) and crossbill (*Loxia curvirostra*)).

One feature of forest plantations that is likely to reduce bird species richness is their lack of structural diversity (well-developed stratification of ground zone, shrub, and lower and upper canopy. A high degree of structural diversity is correlated with high bird species richness, but structural diversity is very low in densely planted monocultures of coniferous forest. There can be no compensation for the loss of bird species associated with grassland, moorland and bog, though careful planting and management can enhance the species richness and structural diversity of conifer forests, increase the number of ecological niches available for occupation by birds and enhance landscape values.

The clash of views over the afforestation of the Flow Country in Sutherland and Caithness has been one of the most vigorous debates on

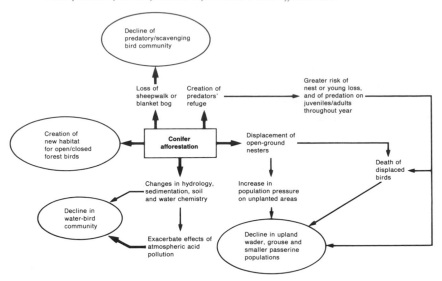

Figure 4.4 Influence of upland afforestation on bird populations: thick lines indicate the relationships have been proven; thin lines indicate probable influences. (Adapted from Thompson D. B. A. *et al.* (1988) in Usher M. B. & Thompson D. B. A. *Ecological change in the uplands*, Blackwell Scientific.)

nature conservation in the UK. The Flow Country contains large areas of blanket peat bog; an Atlantic vegetation type which is poorly represented anywhere else in the world. It has been argued that the extensive nature of the Flows, their near sub-arctic climate, the interesting and rare combinations of blanket bog plant communities and the presence of large numbers of arctic and boreal birds, make them as significant in terms of a wildlife resource as the great nature reserves of continental Europe, such as the Camargue Delta of France. If this is so, surely the case for their conservation has been made? While the Forestry Commission was encouraging the afforestation of the Flows, the Nature Conservancy Council was arguing for its protection and discovering that designating areas as Sites of Special Scientific Interest (SSSIs) offered little protection. If the landowners cannot plant trees, does the nation recompense them for the potential loss of revenue? The answer, surely, must be one of a balance between conflicting interests and the mitigation of adverse impacts as far as is possible.

Conservation and exploitation of biological systems

5.1 Levels of human impact on ecosystems

Before considering the needs for conservation and how ecosystems can be utilised to our long-term advantage, it is necessary to evaluate the impact that people have on ecosystems.

The level of impact on ecosystems should be viewed in relation to the landscape or habitat type that is being affected. A hierarchy of landscape and vegetation types against which impacts could be judged, described in 1971 by V. Westhoff in 'Dynamic structures of plant communities' (In Duffey, E. & Watts, A. S. (eds.) *Scientific management of plant and animal communities for conservation*, Blackwell Scientific), takes into account the degree of intervention in ecosystem processes and the consequences of that intervention on the structure (formation and physiognomy) of the plant communities. They are:

1 *Natural landscape*
   The flora and fauna are uninfluenced by people. (Westhoff suggests that this type no longer occurs in western and central Europe.)

2 *Subnatural landscape*
   The flora and fauna are similar to the potential natural vegetation in species composition and structure (and hence appearance), but the influence of people can be measured.

3 *Semi-natural landscape*
   The plant communities are to a large extent indigenous but the vegetation type has been essentially changed by human activity. The plant communities present a different structure and appearance to the expected natural vegetation. Examples of this in the UK are unimproved grasslands, heathlands and moorlands, which would all be expected to develop into woodland if not managed in some way.

Table 5.1. Two-dimensional matrix assessing the degree of importance of pollution damage (or environmental influence)

Effects of a polluting activity	Targets of a polluting activity				
	1 People	2 Domestic livestock	3 Crops and fisheries	4 Wildlife	5 Pest and disease vectors
I Acute toxicity and death	+ + +	+ + +	+ + +	+ +	Effects may be beneficial but monitoring still required to record scale and nature of effects
II Chronic damage and ultimate death	+ + +	+ + +	+ +	+ +	
III Impaired growth, function and reproduction	+ + +	+ + +	+ +	+	
IV Impaired behavioural response	+ + +	+ + +	+ +	+	

Targets from 1 to 5   Decreasing concern or significance.
Effects from I to IV   Decreasing severity.

+ + +   Effects wholly unacceptable, requiring instant remedy on detection.
+ +   Effect unacceptable on any significant scale, action being required as soon as scale of damage is established.
+   Effects unwelcome, requiring investigation and monitoring with corrective action if on a significant scale and if resources permit.
Source: Holdgate (1977).

4 *Cultivated landscape*

Both the structure and species composition of the vegetation is completely determined by intervention and its use is directed primarily to the production of food or fibre, or for amenity use.

Westhoff's list could be improved by the addition of another category:

5 *Devastated landscape*

This includes landscapes where virtually no vestiges of natural vegetation are left, for example in many urban areas and where industrial processes have left behind a legacy of dereliction.

A second approach to the impact of human activities on biological systems is to rank the impact of pollutants in a two-dimensional matrix which considers:

1 the significance of the target of the pollutant (or environmental influence); and

2 the effects on the target.

This approach (suggested by Holdgate (1977)) neatly encapsulates our concerns for a variety of living systems (see table 5.1).

The logic of this approach in considerations of wider environmental concerns, including landscape and habitat changes, is obvious. It would be easy to add columns for ecosystems, habitats, landscape categories (see above) or even global issues, and to add areas of lesser concern (e.g. effects on aesthetic values) to the rows.

Considerations like those of Westhoff (1971) and Holdgate (1977) are thought-provoking and useful, as they provide a context against which conservation needs and exploitation pressures can be balanced. It is often necessary, however, to make decisions on conservation matters which are based on value judgements as much as on scientific fact. These judgements must be guided by common sense and concern for the long-term health and quality of the environment in which we live, but it is not always possible to assemble sufficient scientific information before decisions have to be made. There are also many occasions where value judgements are the critical features in conservation decision-making processes (see chapter 6). A good example of the dilemma that often faces conservation managers can be seen in the management of Hartlebury Common Nature Reserve in the county of Hereford and Worcester. The common is an area of sandy heathland which was created from acid oak woodland centuries ago by a variety of land-uses. The typical heathland vegetation produced is a vegetation type of high conservation significance in the UK because of its rapid decline in area due to urbanisation and agricultural use. In the absence of stock and rabbit grazing, particularly since the introduction of myxomatosis in the 1950s reduced rabbit numbers, it is necessary to pull up the growing seedlings to prevent the invasion of the heath by tree seedlings of birch (*Betula* spp.), poplar (*Populus* spp.) and oak (*Quercus* spp.). This is what the Hereford and Worcester County Council does, as it is their judgement that the area ought to be conserved as open heathland. Many of the members of the public from the neighbouring town of Stourport, however, were aghast at this decision and felt that nature should be allowed to run its course in a nature reserve.

It is as well to remember here that ecology, as a science, is neutral, and cannot be used to say what is desirable or undesirable. Indeed, there is a need to distinguish between scientific and value judgements, because many of the objectives for ecosystem management are based on judgements about landscape qualities, wildlife values, natural beauty, and so on, that are nearly impossible to quantify.

5.2   Exploitation of natural and artificial ecosystems

The landscape categories (see section 5.1) provide a useful background for examining the exploitation of ecosystems. The main focus for the use of ecosystems by western societies will, of course, relate to the semi-natural and cultivated landscapes, which have been produced as a result of various levels of exploitation. In the past, people have existed by exploiting natural and subnatural landscapes and it is possible to find parts of the world where this is still the case, for example the hunter–gatherer societies of the Indians of the Amazonian tropical rainforests, the Pygmies of western Central Africa and various groups of Aboriginals in the Andaman Isands, west Malaysia, Borneo and the Philippines.

Changes in agricultural practices in the UK have been discussed in chapter 3. The accelerating development of agricultural systems for maximising productivity will no doubt continue, but there has been a recent (1990s) move to concentrate productivity on a smaller area by setting aside some land for low-intensity use. This will obviously create opportunities for conservation if the set-aside area should become significant. How far this development will proceed remains to be seen. With the changes that emerged from the National Parks and Access to the Countryside Act 1949, National Parks, Sites of Special Scientific Interest, Local Nature Reserves, Areas of Outstanding Natural Beauty, National Nature Reserves (82 by 1966) and subsequent developments, for example Environmentally and Nitrate Sensitive Areas (1986) and Set-aside (1987), it is possible that in the UK we are witnessing the beginning of the development of a countryside dichotomy. One part will be used to produce high-quality food from highly productive, high-grade farmland, using high-intensity methods; other large areas will be managed for their traditional landscape qualities as buffer zones between intensive-farming areas and sensitive sites, for organic farming, for production and landscape forestry, for recreation and tourism and for nature conservation. It is very likely that many of the areas not used for intensive agriculture will need to be managed in a traditional way if they are to retain their aesthetic or conservation value. A number of questions must then be asked:

1 Who pays for the management?
2 Should the nation subsidise low-productivity agriculture, and consequently low financial return, for the sake of other benefits and values?
3 Should there be a national policy for rural land use in the UK and other similar societies?

5.3   Necessity for and purposes of conservation

The need for conservation would appear to be self-evident, but it is worth considering the motivating forces behind the increasing interest in and awareness of the subject.

> Any book about the conservation of nature must draw on the experience of a broad range of academic and professional disciplines. This is first because nature is valued by many different groups of people: by countrymen as part of their livelihood; by scientists for research; by resource conservationists for the future; by teachers for education; by naturalists to satisfy their curiosity; and most of us for the opportunities it offers for recreation, for its beauty and for its very naturalness. And second, it is because nature can only be conserved by combining the skills of foresters and agriculturalists, natural and social scientists, economists, journalists, planners, critics, administrators and politicians.
>
> *Warren A. & Goldsmith F. B. (eds.) (1983).*

These views can be applied to wider considerations and take into account environmental concerns relating to resources, pollution and our aesthetic heritage of architecture and landscape. We could easily substitute 'environmental concerns' for 'conservation of nature' in their statement.

It is not possible to find a definition of conservation that satisfies all people; the *Concise Oxford Dictionary* definition of conservation is 'preservation', a definition that only reminds me of a car sticker, which declared, 'Conserve nature, pickle a squirrel'.

Conservation these days means so much more than preservation, but unfortunately it means different things to different people and it is difficult to find a satisfactory, all-embracing definition. In 1964 conservation was defined by E. M. Nicholson ('Orchestrating the use of land', New Scientist **22**:350–1) as the 'management or guidance by man ... of the complex natural processes which sustain life on earth' – a very anthropocentric viewpoint. Frankel and Soulé put it a different way:

> We use the term 'conservation' to denote policies and programmes for the long-term retention of natural communities under conditions which provide the potential for continuing evolution, as against 'preservation' which provides for the maintenance of individuals or groups but not for their evolutionary change.
>
> *Frankel O. H. & Soulé M. E. 1981 Conservation and evolution, Cambridge University Press*

This points out the significance of the conservation of genetic material and the provision of the opportunity for natural selection to operate. Another approach considers conservation to be 'the saving of natural resources for later consumption', which relates the concept to the field of resource utilisation, which would include mineral as well as biological resources. Watts, a biogeographer, raises a number of relevant issues:

> ...it is agreed that the conservation movement undoubtedly seeks to preserve in balance the maximum rates of biological productivity, energy transfer, and chemical element exchange in all ecosystems, while at the same time upholding the quality of the environment and all suited organisms which live therein. To some, it is also explicitly involved in the protection of natural, semi-natural, or aesthetically-pleasing landscapes; to others, it is invoked in the innovation of planning schemes which set precise limits to zones of urban and industrial growth. It should also generate an attitude of mind which encourages man to adopt a constructive and harmonic relationship with his environment.
>
> *Watts D. 1971* Principles of biogeography, *McGraw-Hill (UK)*

Finally I return to some views expressed by Westhoff, who worked in Holland, where domination of the environment is responsible for the very existence of large parts of the country and for the nature of almost all the rest:

> A large number of biotic communities would not be able to persist or even to exist without a major human impact. Nevertheless, many of them require preservation, especially the semi-natural ones. Nature does not need defending against man himself, but against the deterioration caused by modern technical production and cultivation methods, which are levelling down the variety of environmental sites, strongly diminishing the original richness of flora and fauna, and aiming at the maintenance of only a very restricted number of cultivated species.
>
> Contrary to this process and in reaction to it, nature conservation has to maintain and to increase environmental variety.
>
> *Westhoff V. 1971 Dynamic structure of plant communities. In Duffey E. & Watts A. S. (eds.)* Scientific Management of plant and animal communities for conservation, *Blackwell Scientific*

The very fact that efforts are being made to conserve biological systems indicates that we attach considerable importance to them, for a variety of reasons — moral, practical and aesthetic. Since the 1970s, and with accelerating interest and purpose, a specialised field of scientific endeavour, conservation biology, has emerged in response to environmental concerns. Conservation biology has a sound base in ecological and evolutionary methodology and theory, yet is driven most strongly by people interested in solving real problems and turning knowledge and understanding to practical advantage. The aims of conservation biology are:

1 to provide scientific conservation principles;
2 to identify conservation problems;
3 to establish corrective procedures; and

4 to bridge the gap between science and management by making scientists responsive to the conservation problems and managers responsive to biological issues.

The philosophy, fields of study and prospects for the new discipline are wonderfully encapsulated by Western and Pearl (1989). Conservation biologists are concerned with extinctions of species, the viability of individual populations and their genetic potential, the issues of scale of both conservation areas and their management interventions, habitat restoration, species re-introductions and captive propagation, future plant and animal communities, biotechnology and conservation biology, human values, political planning and roles for the developed and developing worlds.

5.4 Objectives of conservation

The practical management of biological systems for conservation has the following objectives:

1 *Species conservation*
It is concerned with the protection of rare, interesting or beautiful species of animals and plants, or the greatest possible variety of species (species richness).

2 *Habitat conservation*
Often widened to include ecosystem conservation, the aim is to maintain a wide variety of habitats.

3 *Conservation as an attitude to land use*
This provides an input into land-use planning and management so that the demands of people on natural or semi-natural systems can be balanced against their ability to support them.

4 *Creative conservation*
Any large-scale modification of the landscape by human activity that presents opportunities for conservation.

It is not difficult to find examples of conservation activities which relate to each of these four objectives. How they are achieved is considered in chapter 6.

Ecosystem management

This chapter is directed at ecosystem management on a *local* (in particular the UK) rather than a global scale. There has been considerable development in the understanding of ecosystem structure and functioning over the last few decades, particularly in the field of vegetation change. In many ecosystems and habitat types it is possible to be reasonably confident about the consequences of management interventions, thus achieving the objectives of management aims. There are a number of important principles which emerge from the problems that face environmental managers.

6.1 Problems of ecosystem management

Ecosystems are in a constant state of flux, but the degree to which and the speed with which changes occur relate to the ecosystem's **successional stage**. Succession is a more or less predictable change in vegetation type. In most of the UK it progresses from bare soil, through annual and biennial weed and grassland communities, to low and then tall scrub. Tall scrub then gives way to pioneer woodland species (e.g. birch (*Betula* spp.), ash (*Fraxinus excelsior*), pine (*Pinus* spp.) and alder (*Alnus glutinosa*)), but the exact nature varies according to environmental factors such as soil and climate. Finally the pioneer canopy species are replaced by tall oak (*Quercus* spp.) forest, the so-called climax type. The stable vegetation types found in fully developed ecosystems (the **climax stage**) change relatively little apart from local variations arising from death and replacement of their constituents. Some community types of considerable conservation interest, for example chalk grassland and heathland, are intermediate stages in the successional process. Their long-term persistence depends on continuing the interruption of the successional series by some form of management intervention. Ecosystems at the initial stages of succession are the most difficult to maintain and are the most easily damaged by mishap or poor management; fortunately they are rarely of conservation interest. Ecosystem managers will need to be aware of the successional processes expected on the site they have to manage.

It is possible to relate management problems to intrinsic factors – those dealing with ecosystem development or management changes within the site itself – and to extrinsic factors – those difficulties arising from influences outside the site. There are not likely to be serious problems arising from dynamic changes where the site contains climax vegetation (e.g. a mature oak (*Quercus* spp.) forest) or where the rate of change is very slow (e.g. a large, undisturbed peat bog).

Intrinsic problems can be categorised under two main headings.

1 Dynamic (or successional) changes

Ecosystems may be difficult to manage because of significant dynamic changes which occur within a short timescale. These may change the vegetation type from one form to another in an entirely natural process (**succession**), yet these may be considered *undesirable* if a plant community with high conservation interest is replaced by a later successional type of less importance. The examples of acid heathland developing into oak woodland, or the short turf of chalk downland being invaded by hawthorn (*Crataegus monogyna*) or juniper (*Juniperis communis*) scrub, could be given here.

2 Land-use changes

Perhaps the most significant problem faced by conservation site managers in developed countries is the situation where the vegetation or even landscape type, has been produced by traditional land-use practices which interrupt the successional series at a **plagioclimax** (or disclimax) state. Any relaxation of the management practices will allow succession to proceed beyond the interrupted stage. Thus, in the UK, the North and South Downs present a uniform landscape created by the destruction of forest cover centuries ago, perhaps as long ago as the late Neolithic period. A vegetation cover dominated by grasses and grassland herbs was maintained by sheep (*Ovis aries*) and rabbit (*Oryctolagus cuniculus*) grazing. In the absence of grazing the grassland is rapidly invaded by hawthorn (*Crataegus monogyna*), elder (*Sambucus nigra*), juniper (*Juniperus communis*), hazel (*Corylus avellana*) and viburnum (*Viburnum opulus* and *V. lantana*) scrub, ash (*Fraxinus excelsior*) trees and eventually develops into beech (*Fagus sylvatica*) woodland. Chalk downland is a vegetation type produced by traditional land-use practices which would disappear if there were marked changes in management. If land managers wish to conserve traditional landscape patterns, then the maxim is to continue with the management interventions that produced it in the first place. This is not always possible because many traditional land-uses are now uneconomic. Much of the downland in the UK is reverting either to scrub (due to the reduction in sheep grazing and the demise of rabbit populations after the introduction of myxomatosis in the 1950s) or, where the soil is deep enough and the slope not too severe, used for the production of cereals.

Extrinsic problems relate entirely to external influences on conservation sites, for example alterations of water tables by drainage in adjacent housing estates. The impact of external factors will have a greater effect on small reserves, long thin sites, or those with convoluted boundaries which have proportionately long margins. In larger sites extrinsic factors can be capitalised on in a creative way by extending the range of environmental influences within the conservation site. External influences may lead to redirection of the course of succession or may alter the existing stability of the ecosystem in undesirable ways.

6.2 Guidelines for ecosystem management

Having recognised the problems that are likely to be encountered by ecosystem managers, are we able to arrive at a set of principles that can be used to guide approaches to their task? In 1966 C. G. van Leeuwen (in *Gorteria* 3 : 16–28) suggested what have been described as six basic rules for ecosystem management. They are re-interpreted here as guidelines rather than rules:

1 Established conservation areas are managed best if the treatment they receive matches as closely as possible the land-use techniques that created the vegetation type in the first place.

2 Managers can take the opportunity of using human activity creatively to develop environmental gradients within conservation sites if they are sufficiently large or robust. On the other hand, fragile plant communities, for example those of unconsolidated sand dunes or rain-fed raised bogs, may have to be protected by the exclusion of human activity.

3 Management operations should be carried out gradually and on a small scale, particularly if they are experimental in nature. If nothing more, this approach will reduce the consequences of a management intervention disaster.

4 More care has to be taken in minimising external influences with small areas because edge effects will be proportionately more significant and their penetration to the centre of the site more likely.

5 In large and robust sites external influences can be capitalised on so that their influence is allowed to develop across its margins. This will allow interaction with internal environmental gradients and enhance environmental richness.

6 Any deleterious external influences should be reduced as far as possible. Any management within the site should be such that induced changes resulting from external influences are prevented or delayed as far as possible.

6.3 Decision-making process

Management plans are the formal record and presentation of the outcomes of management planning processes. They emerge as practical and pragmatic sets of management recommendations from considerations of the objectives of the site. It is important that the problems unique to each site are identified and that the management guidelines (see section 6.2) are borne in mind at all times. Often a great effort is put into the design and development of management plans, but the recommendations in them are frequently ignored and operations not carried out. The reasons for this failure usually relate to a lack of finance and labour for the full implementation of unrealistic plans. This emphasises the necessity of considering all constraints to the implementation of management interventions, not just the biological problems. Many management plans are written as documents reflecting ideals and are of little use in practice. Good plans are always subject to improvements and fine tuning in the light of increasing knowledge and understanding and as a result of changes brought about by management successes and failures.

The process of land-use management planning is shown in figure 6.1. This approach to a decision-making process has been described as the

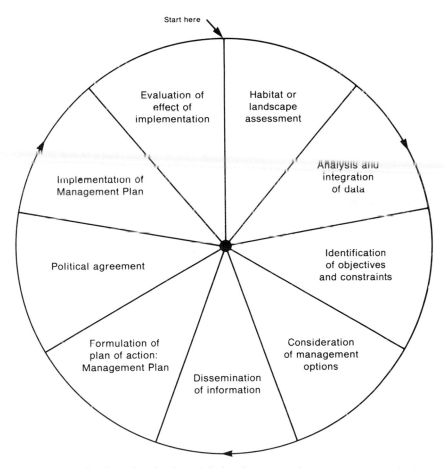

Figure 6.1 The 'bicycle wheel model' for decision-making processes, applied to consideration of land-use management planning decisions.

'bicycle wheel' model – stressing the importance of continual revision of the plan. The information assembled in the early stages of the process should be disseminated and considered by as wide a range of interested parties as possible, so that the decision-making process can be seen to be open and well-informed. The proposition that the implementation of a management plan may be influenced by political decisions is included because the availability of finance to implement schemes is often dependent on political decisions. Management plans should be convincing documents which show that the proposed schemes are necessary, worthwhile and viable.

6.4 Format of management plans

The written product of the decision-making process is the management plan. A fairly consistent format has evolved for this which mirrors the logical approach to the decision-making processes involved. The plans must provide the following information:

1 a record of the features of the conservation site and surrounding areas;
2 a description of the reasons for management and the aims it hopes to achieve;
3 a discussion of ways in which the aims may be fulfilled and a description of why the particular methods that are proposed were chosen;
4 a discussion of possible problems and conflicts that are likely to arise and a consideration of how these may be avoided or their impact reduced; and
5 a prescription of how human and other resources are to be utilised.

Considerations of such information can then be distilled into the format of a management plan. A brief summary of the format developed by the Ecology and Conservation Unit at University College, London, and adopted by most conservation organisations is given in table 6.1.

Needless to say, the inputs to a management plan demand a high degree of technical and scientific knowledge and understanding from a team drawn from a variety of disciplines, for example ecology, land-use planning, cartography and hydrology. The exact significance of each of the contributions will vary depending on the site for which the plan is being developed. A management plan for a small nature reserve could well be written by a handful of people in a few weeks. At the other end of the scale the management plan for the North Yorks Moors National Park was produced in 1977 after 3 years work guided by a consultative committee drawn from 52 different organisations. What is more, substantial reviews of the plan were made in 1984 and 1991. Although the format of this plan does not exactly match that suggested above, the decision-making process, explained in the model earlier, is apparent. This document, with its logical

Table 6.1. Suggested format for the contents of management plans

Parts	Details
Part 1 Description	1.1. General information (location, outline description, tenure) 1.2. Description (all aspects including physical and biological characteristics, land-use history, past management and ecological relationships) 1.3. Bibliography and register of research 1.4. Appendices (including summary table of factual information)
Part 2 Policy and prediction	2.1 Reasons for establishment 2.2. Evaluation of features and site potential 2.3. Objectives (long- and short-term) 2.4. Factors influencing management (constraints due to legal and managerial factors; tenure and access; health and safety; anthropogenic and natural trends; external factors; and impact assessment) 2.5. Specified limits (mainly relating to impact of operations for one objective interacting with others; setting the limits within which interventions can expect to be successful or acceptable)
Part 3 Prescription	3.1. Project register (specific proposals for management interventions) 3.2. Work schedule (a schedule for implementation of the projects) 3.3. Maps (of existing situation, desired state, undesirable trends, and management required)

Source: Wood J. B. & Warren A. 1978 A handbook for the preparation of management plans: Conservation Course Format, revision 2. *Discussion Papers in Conservation,* University College, London.

presentation and sound contents, is a good example of a plan for the conservation management of land on a large scale. Management plans like these make very interesting study documents because they consider such a wide range of physical, biological, cultural and social factors.

6.5   Management techniques

It is not possible to describe all the possible techniques available for use in management interventions. It is, however, important to remember the guiding principles outlined above. A detailed, but by no means exhaustive, account of the practical options available for carrying out specific tasks can be found in Tait *et al.* (1988). Some examples of techniques with wide application are described below.

6.6 Managing grasslands for conservation and amenity purposes

A large proportion of the UK is covered in grass, mainly used for agriculture, but also for amenity, recreation and conservation purposes. Pasturing of stock is a traditional land-use of great antiquity, but in common with most agricultural practices, management of both stock and grass production has changed tremendously this century, particularly in the post-war period (post-1945). In this country the changes have resulted from two factors:

1 the agricultural industry's response to the nation's need to produce large quantities of inexpensive food;
2 the farmers' needs to maximise profits.

Traditional management of grassland was by careful manipulation of grazing stock in order to maintain a balance between grass growth and its utilisation. Some fields were set aside for hay production so that fodder could be stored to feed animals in winter when grass growth was slow. (Fields used for grazing are known as pastures, those used for hay making as meadows.) Fertility of the fields was sustained by the return of animal manure to the land, directly from stock or by muck spreading. Meadows near rivers and streams were often inundated in winter, partly to reduce the immediate consequences of flooding on towns downstream, but also to use the silts deposited in the meadows by flood water to increase soil fertility.

Grassland farming is still a very important and a highly intensive business. Productivity is enhanced by the use of mineral fertilisers (particularly nitrates) and selective herbicides and by establishing swards which consist only of highly productive varieties of a few, or even one, species of grass. The development of silage techniques has enabled spring and summer grass production to be conserved for winter stock feeding and the traditional management of hay meadows has all but disappeared. This has led to the decline in the area of unimproved pastures, which have considerable nature conservation interest because of their species richness. In many areas conservationists have to manage grassland sites without the benefit of grazing animals and are forced to use machinery.

A great deal of research has been carried out on the conservation of grassland sites. There is a strong interaction between frequency and method of cutting (by mower, scythe, flailer or topper machines), the costs of machinery and labour, and conservation objectives. The nature conservation value of grassland is very closely allied to the species richness of the sward, which is usually highest in moderately fertile, closely grazed turf. The competitiveness of grass species is reduced by low fertility of soil and grazing. Sheep grazing produces the highest species richness because it creates a very short turf which favours dwarf perennial herbs. Trampling associated with moderate stocking rates creates opportunities for plants to invade the turf and increase or maintain species richness. The ideal for the conservation manager would be to own a flock of sheep, but this is not often practicable. (The BBONT, however, own and use such a flock for grassland conservation management in Berkshire, Buckinghamshire and Oxfordshire.) The next-best alternative is to mow the grass in such a way as to mimic sheep grazing. The timing of the cut, the nature of the mowing machine and the removal, shredding or leaving of cut grass all have subtle influences on the species composition of grassland. The abundance of false oat grass (*Arrhenatherum elatius*) and cow parsley (*Anthriscus sylvestris*) on road margins throughout the country is thought to be due to their ability to grow through the litter of stems and foliage left by verge mowing. Traditional hay meadow management produces species-rich grassland with only one cut a year and is capable of maintaining species-rich swards in conservation sites.

A further complication in grassland management for conservation is that it is often necessary to carry out management interventions to suit the needs of other wildlife. The corncrake (*Crex crex*) has declined because its nesting and breeding behaviour is disrupted by the early cutting of grass, and this and other grassland breeding birds, for example skylark (*Alauda arvensis*) and lapwing (*Vanellus vanellus*), have been influenced by changes in the agricultural management cycle of grassland. Grassland butterfly populations are dependent on flowers for their nectar supply and the presence of specific host plants for their caterpillars. Management of grassland reserves has to take into account all of these factors.

6.7 Coppicing

Coppicing is a traditional woodland land-use technique (see figure 6.2), which produces long lengths of small-diameter round wood. These were used for making sheep hurdles, fences, wattle-and-daub walls for houses, tool handles, chair legs and backs, for firewood and so on. The species used most frequently for coppice production were chestnut (*Castanea sativa*), hazel (*Corylus avellana*), ash (*Fraxinus excelsior*), hornbeam (*Carpinus betulus*), lime (*Tilia platyphyllos* and *T. cordata*), oak (*Quercus* spp.) and alder (*Alnus glutinosa*). The coppice stems were cut on a rotation of between 8 and 30 years, depending on the species involved and the product required. Coppicing was frequently combined with the production of tall large-diameter timber trees, in the practice of coppice-with-standards. The standards, the canopy trees, were grown at a low density and cut on a much

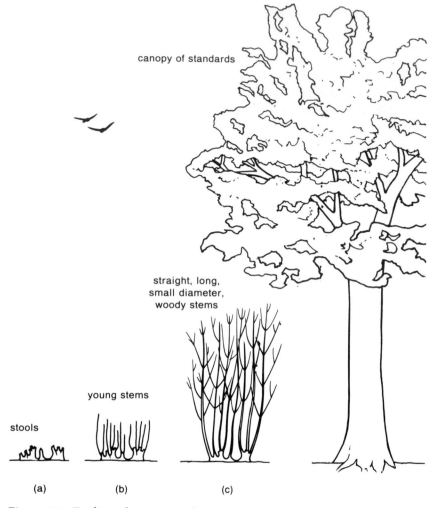

Figure 6.2 Traditional coppice cycle: (*a*) stools cut to ground level, (*b*) after one year's growth, and (*c*) at maturity.

longer rotation (about 60–70 years or more) or harvested individually when required.

Coppicing produced a woodland flora and fauna of considerable conservation interest. Coppicing is rotational in nature and creates a cycle of changing conditions in:

1 structural features (e.g. open woodland, developing scrub and stratified canopy layers);
2 environmental influences (e.g. light penetration, humidity levels and varying levels of competition amongst the plants); and
3 germination conditions (e.g. bare soil, abundant light, darkness and scarification).

Overall, coppicing produces a variety of habitat types and niches, and results in a considerable increase in plant and animal species richness. The disturbance and conditions caused by coppicing allow plants normally associated with woodland edges and paths to penetrate into the centre of the woodland. There is a change in the pattern of bird species utilising a coppice during the cycle. Open glades are used by some birds (e.g. nightjar (*Caprimulgus europaeus*), pied flycatcher (*Ficedula hypoleuca*) and tree pipit (*Anthus trivialis*)), while others prefer the thick cover of the early growth stages (e.g. nightingale (*Luscinia megarhynchos*) and dunnock (*Prunella modularis*)). Many species nest in shrubby coppice stems (e.g. blackbird (*Turdus merula*) and song thrush (*T. philomelos*)), blue tit (*Parus caeruleus*) and coal tit (*P. ater*) feed in the canopies as they develop, and many birds depend on the presence of old standards (e.g. treecreeper (*Certhia familiaris*), nuthatch (*Sitta europaea*)). In a study of nightingales in hornbeam coppice, it was found that bird density was highest where oak standards were present and the coppice was at a particularly bushy stage (5–8 years old). It was unsuitable for nightingales after 15 years. To retain nightingales in a woodland site it is thus necessary to maintain areas of coppice at different growth stages (as is done in Trench and Tidesley Woods near Worcester, close to the northern extremity of the nightingale's distribution range).

6.8   Culling

Culling is the controlled reduction in numbers of an animal population by either removal or killing, for a defined purpose and to a notional pre-determined level. The word 'culling' is used in some places in a wider sense, for example in Scotland it is often used to refer to the harvest of red deer. The main reasons for culling are:

1 to prevent overgrazing and a consequent decline in environmental quality;
2 to produce a grazing intensity suitable for maintaining vegetation at a particular successional stage (the plagioclimax);
3 to maintain the health of the grazing population; and
4 to select superior members and to reduce the proportion of undesirable characters in a population.

6.9   Red deer culling

A substantial amount of research work has been carried out on red deer (*Cervus elephas*) and its interactions with the vegetation on which it feeds. In New Zealand deer have caused damage to the indigenous forests. In the Highlands of Scotland, deer variously harm conifer plantations, provide financial returns from shooting and deer farming and, in places, also cause overgrazing leading to an undesirable change in vegetation and a deterioration in the quality of deer. For all these reasons deer are culled. For culling to be successful, either to control what is a pest or to provide a sustainable yield of deer for shooting and/or venison, considerable scientific knowledge and understanding of deer population dynamics is necessary. Culling operations themselves have provided much useful data on the demography and population processes of red deer.

It appears that grazing of the uplands in Scotland by deer, cattle and sheep increases species richness of the vegetation. Low grazing intensities on the Island of Rhum following the removal of sheep led to a reduction in the number of plant species in grassland and dominance by purple moor grass (*Molinia caerulea*). The deer that were left were then supplemented by the introduction of West Highland cattle in order to reverse the decline in species richness in the herb-rich heaths and grasslands, which contained species such as wild thyme (*Thymus polytrichus*), eyebrights (*Euphrasia* spp.), self-heal (*Prunella vulgaris*), bird's foot trefoil (*Lotus corniculatus*) and yarrow (*Achillea millefolium*). These plants are unable to compete with lank and tall-growing grasses in the absence of grazing.

It is in forest that red deer culling is most necessary in order to prevent damage to the trees. Deer browse on tree foliage and twigs, which reduce growth rates in young trees, especially if the leading shoot is removed. They also strip bark, which causes damage to plantations and may reduce the frequency of preferred trees (e.g. rowan (*Sorbus aucuparia*), willow (*Salix* spp.), ash (*Fraxinus excelsior*) and beech (*Fagus sylvatica*)) in woodland. Ground zone plants, for example heather (*Calluna vulgaris*), are replaced by cowberry (*Vaccinium vitis-idaea*) or bilberry (*V. myrtillus*), and these may give way to wavy hair grass (*Deschampsia flexuosa*) if grazing pressure is very high. Conifer plantations are not free from attack and red deer will feed on silver fir (*Abies alba*), Norway spruce (*Picea abies*) and Sitka spruce (*P. sitchensis*), particularly in winter. It is difficult to keep red deer out of forests, even with a complete ring of deer fencing, so plantations are protected by shooting and designing plantations to facilitate good shooting control. The costs of control can be met by the returns from hunting permits and the sale of venison.

6.10   Other culling operations

Culling is used to reduce the impact of large herbivorous mammals in game parks in Africa. Unchecked population growth of several species has led to considerable damage to plant communities. Elephants (*Loxodonta*) have been culled in the Kabalega Fall National Park in Uganda, the Kruger National Park in South Africa and the Tsavo National Park in Kenya and hippopotamus (*Hippopotomus*) numbers have been reduced in Ruwenzori National Park in Uganda. The control operations were controversial, but the managers of these parks obviously preferred to cull than allow the growing animal populations to cause unacceptable damage to the vegetation. The possibility of long-term damage to the environment's carrying capacity and animal population crashes were also taken into account.

The avocet (*Recurvirostra avosetta*), the emblem of the RSPB (Royal Society for the Protection of Birds), is a bird that occurs in relatively low numbers in the UK. After an absence of about 100 years it started breeding again in East Anglia in 1940. The RSPB maintains reserves, the most notable being Havergate Island and Minsmere, in Suffolk, specifically to encourage avocet colonisation and to increase its population. Two critical features of the management are:

1 the provision of a suitable habitat for feeding and nesting (brackish, but not hypersaline, lagoons in salt marshes); and
2 the control of nest predators (black-headed gull (*Larus ridibundus*) and kestrels (*Falco tinnunculus*)).

The nesting islands and salinity are maintained by careful control of freshwater flows and levels with sluices. The gulls have been successfully controlled by removal of their nests and eggs (see figure 6.3). This has allowed the avocet population increase, which was markedly interrupted by gull predation, to continue.

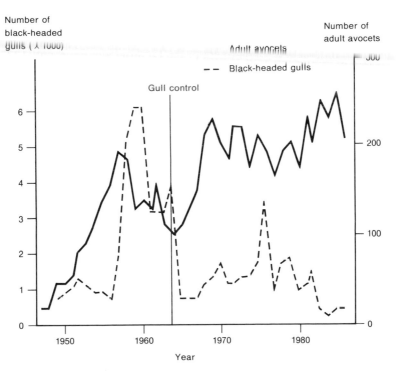

Figure 6.3 The impact of the culling of black-headed gulls on avocets at Havergate Island. (Data from Hill D. (1988) in *Journal of Animal Ecology* **57**:669–83.)

Reclamation of degraded environments

7.1   Principles of reclaiming degraded land

There are large areas of land in the UK which have been rendered derelict by a variety of industrial activities. Dereliction from industrial processes in the UK commenced centuries ago but the rate of dereliction accelerated from the time of the Industrial Revolution (about 1750) onwards. We have a legacy of scarred landscapes resulting from industrial operations, for example wastes from coal mining, the iron and steel industries, and the mining and smelting of non-ferrous metals; toxic wastes from chemical industries; and the quarrying and digging of pits for the extraction of sand, gravel, brick- and china-clay and roadstone. The damage caused by new industries is much more closely regulated, but it was still possible to estimate that the rate of production of derelict land in Britain in 1980 was 1200–1600 hectares per year (Bradshaw and Chadwick (1980)). This figure is matched in some years by the rate of reclamation. Department of the Environment figures for 1982 indicated that over 117 000 hectares of land remained derelict in England, Wales and Scotland.

The dereliction caused by different industries creates different problems for those given the task of repairing the damage, but there are some over-riding principles. The main reasons for carrying out repairs on these degraded environments are:

1   to reduce the unattractiveness of the resulting landscape by creating an environment which has value for amenity, recreation, wildlife, or food or wood production;
2   to introduce a cover of vegetation to regulate run-off of water so that pollution from particulate and dissolved toxic material is not carried into watercourses (i.e. to prevent leakage into neighbouring eco-systems);
3   to introduce a cover of vegetation to stop toxic dust from blowing off the waste material; and
4   to create a vegetation cover to enhance the stability of the slopes of the waste.

Most wastes, to generalise, have a number of features which are not conducive to plant growth:

1 The mineral matrix rarely has a particle-size distribution that would be expected in good soils. They may be stony or with coarse particles, sometimes compacted by heavy machinery, or, less frequently, may consist of large quantities of fine material.
2 They are usually deficient in major plant nutrients, particularly nitrates and phosphates.
3 There is often an imbalance of plant nutrients.
4 Many wastes contain appreciable quantities of toxic ions.
5 The organic content, soil micro-organisms and decomposer systems are often absent or very limited.
6 Wastes are frequently deficient in ion exchange systems which can hold vital plant nutrients within the ecosystem so that they are not lost by leaching.
7 They often have exceptional hydrogen ion (pH) concentrations.

Reclamation is not just a matter of re-establishing a plant cover but creating an integrated, fully-functioning and leak-proof (i.e. a closed nutrient cycle) ecosystem. Land dereliction can be approached, therefore, from the point of view of the repair of a damaged ecosystem (for summary, see figure 7.1). Often the ecosystem may be so damaged that any hope of restoration

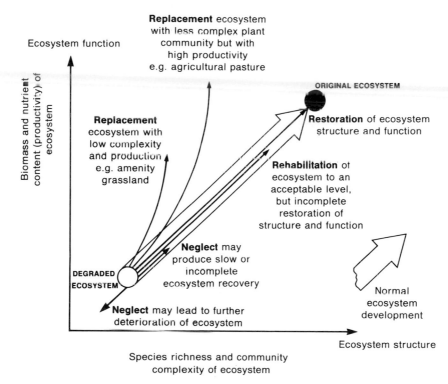

Figure 7.1 The process of repair of degraded ecosystems quantifying ecosystem development in two dimensions — structure and function. (Adapted from Bradshaw A. D. (1984) in *Landscape Planning* **11**:35–48.)

Table 7.1. The underlying problems of derelict land and their treatment

Category	Problem	Immediate treatment	Long-term treatment
Physical			
Structure	Too compact	Rip or scarify	Vegetation
	Too open	Compact or cover with fine material	Vegetation
Stability	Unstable	Stabiliser/mulch	Regrade or vegetation
Moisture	Too wet	Drain	Drain
	Too dry	Organic mulch	Vegetation
Nutrition			
Macronutrients	Nitrogen	Fertiliser	Legume
Micronutrients	Others	Fertiliser + lime	Fertiliser + lime
		Fertiliser	
Toxicity			
pH	Too high	Pyritic waste or organic matter	Weathering
	Too low	Lime or leaching	Lime or weathering
Heavy metals	Too high	Organic mulch or metal-tolerant cultivars	Inert covering or metal-tolerant cultivars
Salinity	Too high	Weathering or irrigation	Tolerant species or cultivars
Plants and animals			
Wild plants	Absent or slow colonisation	Collect seed and sow or spread soil containing propagules or plants	Ensure appropriate conditions
Cultivated plants	Absent	Sow normally or hydroseed	Appropriate after-care
Animals	Slow colonisation	Introduce	Ensure appropriate habitat

Source: Bradshaw A.D. 1983 The reconstruction of ecosystems, *Journal of Applied Ecology* **19**:151–58.

to its original form is not possible in the short term: in this case some measure of the degradation may become permanent, except on a timescale that is geological in extent.

Practical factors that will need attention in the reclamation process are:

1 It is important to know exactly what is preventing the natural re-establishment of a vegetation cover. In some sites local variations in soil properties (e.g. pH, nutrient deficiencies and toxic chemicals) are substantial. In industrially degraded ecosystems it is often found that several factors are limiting to biological productivity. These conditions have to be fully understood before ecosystem repair is attempted.

2 Engineering problems, for example those associated with slope stability, subsidence, contour and drainage, have to be addressed.

3 It is essential that reclaimed land is given adequate attention after the initial stages of reclamation have been successfully undertaken. After-care is necessary until a fully-functioning ecosystem has been re-established, otherwise degeneration will ensue. After-care usually takes the form of regular additions of fertiliser or ameliorating chemicals or other form of management intervention, for example stock grazing.

The basic problems associated with degraded land and suggested treatments are summarised in table 7.1. The different problems of china clay waste, coal waste and land contaminated by heavy metals, together with approaches to their treatments that attempt to repair the damaged ecosystems, are described in sections 7.2, 7.3 and 7.4.

7.2 China clay waste

The china clay extraction industry in the UK is centred principally near St Austell in Cornwall. The china clay (kaolin) is removed by high-pressure water jets from the bottoms and sides of deep pits. For every tonne of china clay extracted, 8 tonnes waste (1 part mica, 1 part undecomposed granite and 6 parts quartz sand) are produced. Since china clay was first extracted in the late eighteenth century the industry has created 10 000 hectares of spoil heaps, clay pits and lagoons. Many of the lagoons are blue and lifeless because of the fine clay particles suspended in the water. The original spoil heaps are cone-shaped, but since the Aberfan disaster, legislation has imposed a more roundly contoured outline to ensure stability of waste tips. (The Aberfan disaster occurred on 21 October 1966, when a coal waste tip slipped and engulfed the Pantglas Infant and Junior School, killing 144 people, mainly children and teachers of the school. The tip had been built on top of a spring and was saturated by heavy rain which had fallen for the two days prior to the disaster.) Research carried out by a team from Liverpool

University, led by Professor A.D. Bradshaw has shown that china clay wastes pose a number of serious problems for plant growth. These are:

1 a deficiency of small-sized soil particles (the clay fraction of normal soils) – the soil consequently being very freely draining and of a low ion exchange capacity;
2 severe deficiencies and an imbalance of major plant nutrients (Ca, N, P, K and Mg) – nitrogen appears to be the most critical limiting factor; and
3 low pH.

Data illustrating the differences in these properties in the china clay wastes, in comparison with those of loam from a relatively poor pasture on nearby Bodmin Moor, are given in table 7.2.

Natural invasion of vegetation on the waste is slow. Initial colonisation is delayed and it takes over 75 years to establish a plant community approaching that of a climax, acid oak woodland (see table 7.3).

As the result of selective agricultural management, a functioning and partly productive ecosystem can be re-established on the wastes within a much shorter time span. The strategies are raising pH levels with lime, increasing the availability of nutrients with fertilisers, maintaining nitrate

Table 7.2. Properties of typical sand and mica and wastes from the china clay industry and a pasture loam from Bodmin Moor

	Wastes		*Bodmin Moor*
Properties	*Sand*	*Mica*	*Loam*
Soil particle size, composition by weight (%)			
Gravel	56	0	0
Coarse sand	30	5	
Coarse and fine sand combined			40
Fine sand	11	44	
Silt	2	47	20
Clay	1	4	40
Plant nutrients, plant available concentration (ppm)			
K	10	13	110
Mg	16	20	71
Ca	85	115	880
P	2.0	2.8	42
N	9	18	1275
pH	4.5	4.0	4.2*

* A pH value of 4.2 is very acid for pasture; a value around pH 6.5 is considered a more satisfactory figure.
Source: Bradshaw & Chadwick (1980).

Table 7.3. Summary of the dominant plants in successional sequence and time scale of invasion of plants on china clay waste

Successional sequence	Dominant plants	Time scale after tipping ceases (years)
Pioneer communities		
Either:	Tree lupin (*Lupinus arboreus*)	} 10
	Yorkshire fog (*Holcus lanatus*)	
Or:	Heather (*Calluna vulgaris*)	
	Gorse (*Ulex eurupaeus* and *U. gallii*)	} 30–40
	Broom (*Cytisus scoparius*)	
Scrub	Grey willow (*Salix cinerea*)	} 50–60
community	Sheep's sorrel (*Rumex acetosella*)	
Woodland	Birch (*Betula* spp.)	
community	Oak (*Quercus* spp.)	
	Rhododendron (*Rhododendron ponticum*)	} 75+
	Hazel (*Corylus avellana*)	
	Ivy (*Hedera helix*)	
	Honeysuckle (*Lonicera periclymenum*)	

production in the soil with legumes and increasing the ion exchange capacity of the soil with the gradual build-up of humic material derived from the plants that have become established. Many of the reclamation schemes in the St Austell area have aimed at the production of grassland from the wastes. This can then be used for low intensity agriculture, providing the slopes are not too steep.

In practical terms the spoil is treated with a series of specialised techniques:

1 The contours are modified with heavy machinery so that they match the natural landscape pattern of the surrounding area. The spoil receives any necessary civil engineering interventions.
2 The waste is treated with lime ($1000 \, kg \, ha^{-1}$) to reduce pH.
3 A mulch of peat or woodpulp is mixed with a special seed mix, and sprayed (hydroseeded) onto the slopes. The seed mix contains:
    (a) species used to create a rapid cover (e.g. perennial ryegrass (*Lolium perenne*)),
    (b) species which will fix nitrogen in acid soils (e.g. red clover (*Trifolium pratense*), white clover (*T. repens*) and bird's foot trefoil (*Lotus corniculatus*)),
    (c) grass species which are tolerant of acid, droughty and nutrient-deficient soils (e.g. red fescue (*Festuca rubra*), sheep's fescue (*F. ovina*) and bents (*Agrostis* spp.)).

The varieties of the species used are those best adapted to the conditions found in the waste.

4 Mineral fertiliser (100 parts N: 60 parts P: 70 parts K) is added (rate 100 kg ha^{-1}) with the hydroseeding mulch. More fertiliser than this would inhibit the germination of the legumes and inhibit the fixation of nitrogen by the developing sward. Further fertiliser is added (rate 500 kg ha^{-1}) after germination. Fertiliser application to unvegetated waste leads to losses of the applied nutrients. This does not happen if a vegetation cover is present to take them up.

5 The grass sward is managed by regular applications of nitrogen-rich fertiliser. The competitive nature of the grasses is reduced by sheep grazing (Soay sheep, a race tolerant of poor pasture, have been used). Grazing allows the slower-growing legumes to persist in the pasture and provide a continuous nitrogen supply to the whole plant community. Successful growth of legumes requires an adequate level of soil phosphate (added in the fertiliser mix).

Where the slopes are too steep for agricultural management and where coarser-grained wastes are too droughty for pasture legumes to persist, the end point of the reclamation process could be a scrub cover of tree lupins (*Lupinus arboreus*) and/or gorse (*Ulex* spp.), then willow (*Salix cinera*) and eventually oak (*Quercus* spp.) woodland. There is little doubt that the initial lag in the colonisation of the wastes by natural processes would be avoided by the amendment/fertiliser/hydroseeding approach. It would also be possible to directly seed or plant tree species, accompanied by tree lupins (*L. arboreus*) (to supply nitrogen), and compress the successional pattern into a much shorter time span than the natural process would follow.

7.3 Coal wastes

The variability of waste material for reclamation is best exemplified in coal wastes. Geological variation in the nature of coal is considerable. Some coal measures associated with limestone strata produce waste material with a more or less neutral pH, but many coals have high sulphur contents, in the form of iron pyrites (FeS_2). Iron pyrites oxidises to sulphuric acid (H_2SO_4) and produces a very low pH.

$$4FeS_2 + 15O_2 + 14H_2O \rightarrow 4Fe(OH)_3 + 16H^+ + 8SO_4^{2-}$$

Low pH levels in waste cause very severe problems by inducing shortages of calcium, phosphate and molybdenum and by mobilising toxic concentrations of a number of cations. Those of greatest significance are aluminium and manganese, but zinc, copper, lead, iron and magnesium also cause difficulties in some wastes. Seams within a colliery may have been laid down in different geological strata, with quite different chemical properties, resulting in a hotchpotch of difficulties. This variation must be known before reclamation starts so that appropriate treatments can be used. Should sulphur-rich waste catch fire (spontaneous combustion is not infrequent on coal spoil tips), the iron pyrites will be oxidised, the sulphur given off as sulphur dioxide (SO_2) and the acidification problem will have been eliminated. In the absence of fire, there is a potential long-term source of acidification in pyrites-rich wastes. It has been calculated that additions of ground limestone of at least $100\,000\,kg\,ha^{-1}$ are necessary to combat potential acid production in some pyritic coal shales. Limestone can produce further problems for plant growth by reducing the availability of phosphates under alkaline conditions. It would seem that some coal waste presents almost intractable difficulties for reclamation.

As is typical with many wastes, coal spoil heaps are deficient in nitrogen and phosphorus and generally have a poor soil particle size distribution. It is possible to restore coal spoil, but the process requires careful planning and a detailed chemical analysis of the nature and variation of the waste. Heavy machinery can be used to bury the most intractable material, landscape the site and rip compacted material. Lime is incorporated in the soil to a depth of 20–50 cm, nutrient deficiencies are moderated with fertilisers and plants adapted to poor soils and acid conditions seeded in. Legumes are an important component of any seed mix because of their ability to fix atmospheric nitrogen. However, heavy lime applications can cause difficulties by fixing phosphate and making it unavailable for plant growth. This is a particular problem with pasture legumes (e.g. white clover (*Trifolium repens*)), so acid tolerant legumes (e.g. bird's foot trefoil (*Lotus corniculatus*)) should be used.

This rather simplified account gives little insight into the difficulties of reclaiming coal wastes. Successful schemes require a large initial investment of finance and the expertise of engineers and ecologists, followed by careful management and after-care.

7.4   Wastes contaminated by heavy metals

Heavy metals are metallic elements with density greater than $5\,g\,cm^{-3}$; the most significant of these in biological terms are cadmium, chromium, cobalt, copper, iron, lead, manganese, mercury, molybdenum, nickel, silver, tin and zinc. A number of these are essential elements for living organisms, but are found only in trace concentrations in living tissue (e.g. Cu, Fe, Mn, Mo and Zn). In high concentrations these elements are toxic. All occur in most soils at low concentrations, but occur in high concentrations in parent ores, mine and smelter wastes. Toxicity problems also arise from other activities, for example electroplating, heavy metal accumulation in sewage sludge, zinc beneath galvanised fences and pylons, lead at rifle targets and clay pigeon butts, and copper in soil from the use of Bordeaux Mixture fungicide. Heavy

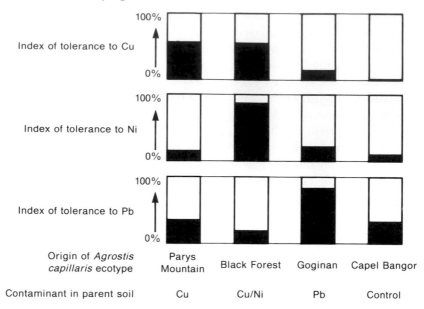

Figure 7.2 The index of tolerance to metals of four ecotypes (including one control ecotype) of common bent grass (*Agrostis capillaris*) from sites contaminated by different metals. An index of tolerance of 100% would indicate no inhibition of growth, 0% no growth at all, compared with the ecotype's growth rate in normal conditions. The ecotypes are only tolerant of the metals found on the sites from which they were collected. (Data from Jowett D. (1958) in *Nature* **182**:816–17.)

metals may be responsible for dereliction of land and an absence of plant growth for centuries following the demise of the industry.

There are few habitats created by nature or by humans that have no life in them. Some plants, **obligate metallophytes**, only occur in soil with relatively high levels of heavy metals. For example the violet *Viola calaminaria*, is only found in areas with high zinc concentrations. An increasingly large number of species of plant, particularly amongst the grass and legume families, have been found to produce **ecotypes** (strains), that are able to grow in contaminated soil. This ability to produce heavy metal tolerant ecotypes has been considered as one of the best examples of evolution in action.

The heavy metal tolerance developed by these plants is highly specific; tolerance to one metal does not produce tolerance to others (see figure 7.2), unless the response has been produced in soils where more than one toxic metal is present. The degree of tolerance found in plants is also directly related to the concentration of the metal in the soil they occur in (see figure 7.3). These facts are indicative of:

1   the presence in plants of metal-specific mechanisms for dealing with the toxicity (this appears to be mediated by the cell wall); and
2   control of the mechanism by several genes.

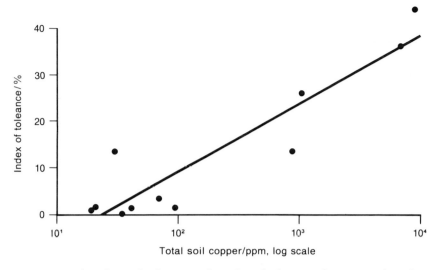

Figure 7.3 The relationship between the index of tolerance of ecotypes of monkey flower (*Mimulus guttatus*) and the concentration of copper in the sites from which they were collected. (Adapted from Allen R. & Sheppard P. M. (1971) *Proceedings of the Royal Society* **B 172**:177–96.)

Other interesting characteristics of heavy metal tolerant plants are:

1 They occur in discrete populations where the specific metal occurs, but they are rare in normal populations. The exclusion of metal-tolerant plants from normal soils is due to the superior competitive abilities of fast-growing non-tolerant ecotypes. The tolerant ecotypes use the toxic wastes as a refuge from this competition.

2 It appears that most plants do not have the potential to develop this tolerance.

3 In comparison with normal ecotypes, tolerant ecotypes have smaller flowers, smaller leaves, thinner stems and tend to be dwarf or prostrate (all adaptations found in plants growing in harsh conditions).

4 Tolerant ecotypes are often less susceptible to nutrient deficiencies than normal plants.

There are four broad approaches to reclaiming land made derelict by heavy metals.

1 Isolate the toxic material by covering with inert waste and then topsoil

This is effective but very costly. Sometimes, heavy metals migrate up through the soil and ultimately cause reclamation schemes to fail. Sublethal quantities of heavy metals in pasture can lead to their accumulation in animal tissue at concentrations considered unsafe for consumption.

Table 7.4. Concentrations (ppm) of plant available metals in copper and zinc smelter wastes, in the Lower Swansea valley, treated with domestic refuse and sewage sludge

Waste	Control	Domestic refuse	Sewage sludge
Copper waste			
Cu	2 040	510	310
Zinc waste			
Zn	16 750	12 370	6 590
Pb	4 350	3 170	780

Source: Gemmell R.P. 1977 *Colonization of industrial wasteland,* Edward Arnold.

2   Allow natural leaching and weathering to reduce concentrations in surface layers

This may pollute drainage water and take decades or even centuries before levels are low enough for plant growth.

3   Ameliorate soil properties with additives

Organic material has the potential to chelate (bind) heavy metals and reduce their availability in soil. Large quantities of organic material (e.g. sewage sludge, peat and domestic refuse) can be mixed with waste for this purpose and produce remarkable reductions in available metal levels (see table 7.4).

The levels of organic material must be maintained by continued additions, either from outside the developing ecosystem or from biological productivity within it, otherwise it will decompose and release the metals into solution.

It is also possible to use chemical amendments for reducing toxic metal concentrations. In chromate smelter wastes iron(II) sulphate ($FeSO_4$) additions precipitate out chromium ions as chromium(III) sulphate ($Cr_2(SO_4)_3$). The iron(II) sulphate ($FeSO_4$) is obtained as a by-product of the manufacture of titanium(IV) oxide (TiO_2). The availability of many toxic metal ions is reduced at high pH levels, so liming is used frequently in treating wastes. This has an added bonus as calcium ions act in an antagonistic fashion to heavy metal toxicity. Metals in calcium-rich spoils show a lower toxicity than would be expected from their concentrations.

4   Re-vegetate with tolerant species or ecotypes

Obviously the plants to use are those with the highest tolerance to the metal in the particular waste and to any other limiting factors present. It has been demonstrated that vegetation can be established on heavily contaminated sites provided tolerant populations are used and suitable fertilisers are added.

Table 7.5. Cultivars of grass species suitable for seeding wastes contaminated by heavy metals

Metal wastes	Cultivar and common name
acid zinc wastes	*Agrostis capillaris* cv *Goginan* (common bent)
calcareous lead/zinc wastes	*Festuca rubra* cv *Merlin* (red fescue)
copper wastes	*Agrostis capillaris* cv *Parys* (common bent)

Seed of a number of tolerant cultivars are available for this purpose (see table 7.5).

With any of these approaches, once a complete vegetation cover has been established, it is vital that the vegetation is given adequate after-care. This means fertiliser applications have to be continued so that the vegetation continues to grow and the nutrient capital of the ecosystem builds up. Eventually the nutrient cycle will be closed and leakage of both desirable plant nutrients and undesirable toxic metals will cease. This may take several decades. The successful reclamation of a degraded landscape must be one of the most satisfying outcomes of the application of the science of ecology for the practitioners involved.

Further reading

Bradshaw A. D. & Chadwick M. J. 1980 *The restoration of land. The ecology and reclamation of derelict and degraded land*, Blackwell Scientific Publications.

Briggs D. J. & Courtney F. M. 1989 *Agriculture and environment. The physical geography of temperate agricultural systems*, Longman Scientific and Technical.

Elsom D. 1987 *Atmospheric pollution. Causes, effects and control policies*, Basil Blackwell.

Freedman B. 1989 *Environmental ecology. The impacts of pollution and other stresses on ecosystem structure and function*, Academic Press.

Holdgate M. 1977 *A perspective on environmental pollution*, Cambridge University Press.

Mabberley D. J. 1991 *Tropical rain forest ecology*, Blackie and Son.

Mannion A. M. 1991 *Global environmental change. A natural and cultural environmental history*, Longman Scientific and Technical.

Mason C. F. 1981 *Biology of freshwater pollution*, Longman.

Moss B. 1988 *Ecology of fresh waters. Man and medium*, Blackwell Scientific Publications.

Nix J. 1991 *Farm management pocketbook*, Wye College, University of London.

Schlesinger W. H. 1991 *Biogeochemistry; an analysis of global change*, Academic Press.

Tait J. *et al.* 1988 *Practical conservation*, Open University in association with the Nature Conservancy Council.

Warren A. & Goldsmith F. B. (eds.) 1983 *Conservation in perspective*, John Wiley.

Wellburn A. 1988 *Air pollution and acid rain. The biological impact*, Longman Scientific and Technical.

Western D. & Pearl M. 1989 *Conservation for the twenty-first century*, Oxford University Press.

Wyman R. L. (ed.) 1991 *Global climate change and life on earth*, Routledge, Chapman & Hall.

Up-to-date information on the subject material of this book appears regularly in the *New Scientist*. More extensive reviews appear in the *Scientific American*.

Index